# CORRECTIONAL OFFICER

## Resource Guide

American Correctional Association

# Acknowledgments

The American Correctional Association wishes to thank the following people for their significant contributions to this publication: Kevin W. Ashburn; Robert Brutsche, M.D.; William C. Collins; James D. Henderson; Robert Levinson, Ph.D.; and Edward E. Rhine, Ph.D.

## *Photo Credits*

The American Correctional Association would like to credit the following for providing photographs for this publication. All other photos are from ACA files.

Blount, Inc. (page 46)
Bucks County Correctional Facility, Doylestown, PA (36, 79)
California Department of Corrections (3, 126)
Capitol Communication Systems, Inc. (16, 115)
Centers for Disease Control, Atlanta, GA (86)
Colorado Territorial Correctional Facility, Canon City, CO (114)
Correctional Medical Systems, Inc. (88, 91)
Correctional Service Canada (25, 128)
Michael Dersin (28, 29, 31, 39, 41, 42, 75, 83, 116, 121, 122)
Eastman Kodak, Inc. (113)
Federal Staff Training Center, Glynco, GA (56)
Florida Department of Corrections (2, 5, 37)
Tom Freeman, AP/Wide World Photos (60, 63, 64)
Georgia Department of Corrections (32)

Henningson, Durham and Richardson, Inc. (21, 24)
Insulgard Corporation (62)
Larimer County Detention Facility, Ft. Collins, CO (104)
Jerry Losik/Syska & Hennessy (35)
Mellon Stuart Co. (112)
Mid-Orange Correctional Facility, Warwick, NY (30)
New York City Department of Corrections (9, 15, 125)
Oklahoma Department of Corrections (52)
Otisville Correctional Facility, Otisville, NY (73)
Pennsylvania Department of Corrections (127)
PHP Healthcare, Inc. (90)
Richmond Times-Dispatch, Richmond, VA (27)
David Singer, Prison Fellowship Ministries (96, 98)
David Skipper (10, 17, 55, 66)
South Carolina Department of Corrections (51, 59, 69, 103, 122)
Stephen Steurer, Correctional Education Association (109, 111)
Szabo Correctional Services (105)
David Texada, Daily Town Talk, Alexandria, LA (67)
UNICOR (110, 118)
U.S. Penitentiary, Marion, IL (45)
Wichita County Detention Center, Wichita Falls, TX (117)

Publications Director: Patricia L. Poupore
Contributing Editor: Richard L. Phillips

Project Editor: Ann Dargis
Editorial Assistant: Marie G. Unger

# Contents

Preface ............................................................................................... iv

Foreword ............................................................................................ v

Introduction ....................................................................................... 1

1. Overview of the Criminal Justice System and the Role of Corrections ........... 4
2. Officers' Responsibilities and Training .................................................. 8
3. Corrections and the Law .................................................................. 12
4. Inmate Supervision and Discipline ...................................................... 20
5. Security and Control ....................................................................... 34
6. Firearms, Gas, and Use of Force ......................................................... 50
7. Emergency Plans and Procedures ........................................................ 58
8. Food Service ............................................................................... 70
9. Sanitation and Hygiene ................................................................... 76
10. Health Care ................................................................................ 82
11. Mentally Ill Inmates ...................................................................... 94
12. Reception, Orientation, and Classification of Inmates ............................. 102
13. Programming and Related Services ..................................................... 108
14. Parole and Release ........................................................................ 120
15. Public Relations and Citizen Involvement ............................................. 124

Index ............................................................................................... 130

ACA Code of Ethics .............................................................................. 132

# Preface

This is the third printing of the *Correctional Officer Resource Guide* issued by the American Correctional Association in 1983. This edition is updated with the most recent third edition ACA standards. It has been prepared to help new and currently employed correctional officers understand the scope and importance of their duties, and the important impact that correctional officers have on institutional operations and individual inmate conduct.

The material included in this publication reflects new attitudes in the correctional field toward inmate supervision, as well as requirements set by the courts and ACA standards for the operation of adult correctional institutions. Those standards, in particular, reflect the progress that has occurred in corrections in recent years, and provide an excellent basis for continued professional employee development and positive change in institutional operations.

# Foreword

This *Correctional Officer Resource Guide* is a product of the expertise and professional background of a number of correctional administrators throughout the country. Its purpose is to provide new correctional staff with a picture of institutional operations—not a complete picture by any means, but a glimpse of the complexity of modern prison operations and the professionally accepted ways of managing them. The core chapters focus on security and inmate supervision procedures, but the guide also contains a wealth of introductory information on other important areas that affect correctional officers in the day-to-day performance of their duties.

This is a particularly appropriate time to update this publication. The late 1980s have been a time of rapid change and tremendous pressure on correctional staff and administrators. Unprecedented growth during the last 10 years has almost doubled the number of people behind bars in the United States, and those upward trends appear to stretch well into the '90s. Fortunately, the public and various legislative bodies are finally beginning to understand the importance of corrections and the need for devoting additional resources to confinement operations. New institutions under construction will add tens of thousands of new prison beds, and a new surge of correctional officers is being hired to staff these institutions. This publication aims to benefit primarily these new staff. It contains valuable information not only for the professional development of new officers, but for currently employed officers and others working directly with inmates.

Information in this publication is consistent with the standards of the American Correctional Association, and they will be referenced in various places throughout the guide. The standards are a set of statements about practical, achievable institutional

policies, procedures, and operations. They represent today's best thinking about how a correctional institution should be organized and operated. If an institution is complying with these standards, then after certain procedures have been followed, it may be accredited—that is, certified as meeting the standards.

Accreditation is increasingly seen as the key to having an effective institutional operation, and also as an avenue for national recognition of high standards of performance at the institutional level. Correctional officers may find it useful to have access to the most recent *Standards for Adult Correctional Institutions*; if a copy cannot be obtained at the local institution, then a copy may be requested from the American Correctional Association for a small fee.

Finally, in reading this publication, it is important to remember that each correctional system has its own specific regulations and policies, and each institution has design differences that create different operational procedures. A publication like this one can describe only the general principles and ideals around which individual facilities shape their security and programs. The procedures and policies described here may not be in effect in a particular institution, or may conflict for good reason with established agency policy or local statutory requirements. In those instances, local regulations and laws must govern the actions of the individual employee. Even so, this guide is a valuable introductory resource, and when used in connection with the training provided by an individual correctional institution or agency, it can be the basis for an excellent understanding of the fundamentals of modern correctional practice.

*James A. Gondles, Jr.*
Executive Director
American Correctional Association

# Introduction

Correctional operations in America are shaped by a changing balance in our society—the balance between the public's right to be free from crime and fear of crime, inmates' rights as they are constantly redefined by the courts, and available resources. As time passes, the balances shift, and corrections must shift with them.

In recent years, the shift has been tied to a continuing increase in crime, and the resulting public reaction. The late 1980s have seen prison populations soar to all-time highs due to increased drug trafficking, heightened enforcement efforts, and various changes in laws and sentences. Public feelings about crime and punishment are, in effect, leading the court system to use the prison options more often. As a result, during the past decade the nation's adult prison population has more than doubled; by the end of 1990, it had reached over 710,054 (Bureau of Justice Statistics).

And so the institutional counts go up, and because these population increases have not been matched by the necessary prison construction and expansion, overcrowding in correctional institutions is now a major concern. In many prisons, two or more inmates are forced to live in cells designed for only one, others live in crowded double-bunked dormitories, or in hallways, dayrooms, and other areas not designed as living quarters. As correctional institutions become more crowded, many inmates who should be confined in single cells because of their violent backgrounds are instead in dormitories, dramatically increasing the chance for problems. Under such conditions, the other physical limits of an institution become more pronounced. Support facilities, such as gymnasiums, kitchens, dining rooms, industries, and medical facilities, are severely stressed. In many cases, program resources are inadequate for the increased numbers of inmates they must serve. Perhaps most importantly, inmate/staff ratios have resulted in less supervision, reduced security, and increased stress in many institutions.

The inmate profile of today's prisons contributes to the problem. American correctional institutions are populated primarily by young, unmarried males. Although there has been a 130 percent increase in the last year, female inmates still make up only 6.7 percent of the entire inmate population in the United States. Inmates are mainly from the lower social and economic strata of society. They are frequently the products of broken homes, poorly educated, unskilled, and possessing unstable work histories.

At the end of 1990, the last year for which complete figures are available, the prison population was approximately 50.6 percent white, 36 percent black, and 8 percent Hispanic (*1991 Corrections Yearbook*). Typical inmates are apt to have a prior criminal record and low self-esteem, and to be uncommitted to any major goals in life. Material failure in a culture firmly oriented toward material success is the most common denominator among them.

Correctional institutions also incarcerate a disproportionate share of individuals who are mentally deficient, emotionally unstable, or prone to violent and other socially deviant behavior. In addition, some special groups within the general prison population are, for a variety of reasons, especially prone to causing problems. Prison gangs, which have been more widespread in recent years, are often formed along racial or ethnic lines, and are increasingly sophisticated, as they align themselves with outside religious or political groups. Revolutionary organizations, with their terrorist tactics, have continued to be active in some institutions; their influence, as well as that of prison gangs, has occasionally become a threat to ex-inmates and their families, as well as correctional staff. Dealing

with these various types of inmates is a tremendous challenge.

The other visible sign of a shifting balance has been in the legal area. Throughout the last several decades, police practices were under close review by state and federal courts; the right to privacy, search and seizure practices, pre-arraignment procedures, and investigative techniques employed by law enforcement agencies were questioned, and at times redefined, by the legal process. Today, it is corrections that is attracting a great deal of interest and concern that had been given in the past to law enforcement. Many correctional agencies themselves are acknowledging problems and attempting system-wide improvements.

Finally, the involvement of the courts, communities, and other decision makers also influences the daily activities of the correctional employee. Many correctional systems are operating under some type of court order or supervision. Others are managed by court-appointed "Special Masters." Still others have formally agreed to make specific changes in order to avoid further court cases. In systems throughout the country, individual institutional staff are being sued by inmates for alleged violations of their rights. Taken together, the

impact that these legal forces are having on prisons is very significant.

The institutional world, with its many varieties of inmates and inmate groups, is often very strange to new correctional staff. The changing demands of the legal system are equally difficult to understand and master. It is important that officers know how to do the technical part of their job well, understand the nature of the inmate population, develop the skills to accurately assess inmate behavior, and be able to react quickly and appropriately to situations. At the same time they have to maintain a high level of professional conduct that is consistent with the courts' demands.

## The Correctional Officer

Well-informed, properly supervised correctional personnel form the foundation for an effective security program, one that can prevent many prison problems. Since correctional officers, along with inmate work supervisors, have the most contact with inmates, their knowledge and competence in security techniques, their powers of observation, and their insight into inmate behavior are of great importance. In addition, since inmates rely on officers for supervision, direction, and information, correctional officers must be well-informed about the institution's policies, programs, and procedures.

There may have been a time when some people thought the way to be a successful correctional officer was through muscle and the sheer weight of unquestioned authority. However, today's correctional setting requires far more. Detailed, written regulations and policy manuals are replacing hunches and instincts as a basis for action. Technology now plays an important part in security. Officers must constantly be aware of new inmate rights and staff responsibilities, because their decisions are increasingly subject to review by the courts, correctional administrators, legislators, and the general public. These are some of the reasons why standards of professional conduct have been developed and are continually being refined—to provide the necessary guidance to agencies in setting up their institutional operations and supervising their staff.

Training is critical in maintaining a professional work force. Correctional officers who are thoroughly trained in technical and interpersonal skills can handle responsibilities and emergencies calmly; and they are more likely to respond quickly and efficiently to urgent situations. Training, combined with experience, will help staff react appropriately to the many kinds of problems and issues that will confront them in their day-to-day duties.

This publication cannot describe an entire training program for correctional officers. Most agencies have a predetermined training program, either at the local institution or at a central training academy, and each employee should take full advantage of all agency resources. However, if the following topics are not covered in the agency's training program, then additional study would be very helpful for the individual officer in dealing with inmates:

• *Causes of criminal or deviant behavior*—Correctional officers who understand why people act in antisocial or deviant ways are better prepared to manage difficult inmates and to be objective in their actions.

• *Understanding minorities*—The disproportionately large percentage of minorities and the relatively high number of white correctional officers in many institutions often lead to severe problems and tensions. Staff should develop an understanding of cultural, social, and ethnic differences within their inmate population, as reflected in language, appearances, gestures, and value systems. Hostility between inmates of different races is common in today's correctional institutions. Thus, a correctional officer's career development should include courses on human behavior, interpersonal relationships, group dynamics, and the effects of cultural differences on behavior.

• *Inmate rights*—State and federal court decisions have increasingly extended offenders' constitutional rights, providing them expanded civil rights, due process, and equal protection under the law. An awareness of the rights of those confined, as well as the rights and responsibilities of correctional staff, will reduce the possibility of tension in the correctional facility.

The basic tasks required of correctional officers have not changed over the years—security inspections, inmate searches, observation and supervision of groups, and marksmanship. To these skills has been added the use of new technologies in newly designed institutions. But the same interpersonal skills and humane attitudes that made good correctional officers in the past make good

correctional officers today. Even if there were no intervention by court officials, no public demand for accountability, no greater recognition of the rights of the confined, and no changing prison population, good correctional practice would still focus our attention on the basics of security and supervision and emphasize humane performance of these duties.

3

# 1

# Overview of the Criminal Justice System
# And the Role of Corrections

The criminal justice system in the United States involves a number of very different organizations carrying out the process of identifying, arresting, detaining, accusing, trying, convicting, and punishing people who have broken the law, at the city, county, state, and federal levels.

## Components of the Criminal Justice System

The four primary components of the criminal justice system are law enforcement, the prosecution, the courts, and corrections.

### Law Enforcement

Law enforcement agencies are primarily responsible for crime prevention, investigation of criminal activities, and apprehension of offenders; they generally ensure public order. State and federal law enforcement agencies in particular also have the responsibility for enforcement of regulatory provisions of the law, in addition to the criminal code. In larger jurisdictions, good community relations are emphasized as an aid in crime prevention.

### Prosecution

The prosecutory agencies, typically the Office of the District Attorney at the state and local level, or Office of the U.S. Attorney at the federal level, are involved in the criminal justice process from the time of arrest to sentencing. These agencies are responsible for determining the actual nature of criminal or regulatory complaints first identified by enforcement agencies. They determine how the law may apply to the particular set of facts, and the likelihood that a successful prosecution will result if the case is pursued.

Prosecutors represent the government in the preparation and presentation of the case to the courts. Where appropriate, they conduct plea negotiations, where the offender agrees to plead guilty before trial, usually in exchange for recommendation for a lesser sentence, and they also present the evidence if the case goes to trial. The prosecutor can make recommendations to the court on the sentence to be imposed on the offender.

### Courts

Criminal courts' structure depends on the jurisdiction involved. Their function may be restricted to processing or judging matters involving minor criminal offenses, traffic violations, and other local ordinance violations. In the case of state and federal courts, they may act on all cases relating to state or federal codes. The court system also includes appeal and supreme courts, which hear appeals from the lower courts. The U.S. Supreme Court is the final level of appeal for all cases, although very few cases ever reach that level.

### Corrections

The corrections part of the criminal justice system generally refers to three major functions: probation, confinement, and parole. This component of the system is responsible for carrying out the sentences the court imposes.

Probation is a sentence that permits the offender to remain in the community under certain specified

4

conditions. The offender is assisted and supervised in the community by a probation officer. If an offender violates any conditions of probation, the court may choose to revoke the probation and place the offender in confinement as specified in the original sentence. Probation may also be imposed without a finding of guilt, usually in the case of a first offender with a minor crime. Upon completion of this kind of probation in a satisfactory manner, the offender will have no record of conviction. If violated, the trial process may be used to follow the case through to a conviction and possible confinement.

Confinement facilities include jails, prison camps, correctional institutions, and prisons or penitentiaries. In many cases, laws also include halfway houses, restitution centers, and similar programs in the confinement category of corrections. Jails tend to be managed by local government, with the sheriff or other local official as the primary administrator. The role of the jail is to hold pretrial and pre-sentence detainees, and those convicted and sentenced to relatively short terms (often under one year). Work and study release programs are also sometimes operated out of jails, in which inmates live in the jail but are permitted to leave for school or work during the day.

Halfway houses are also a form of confinement, generally used for minimum-security inmates about to complete their sentences. These centers, usually located near or in the community where the inmate is about to be released, provide housing, job placement assistance, drug and alcohol counseling, and other services. They generally help the inmate make the change from institutional life to the free world. Halfway houses are also sometimes used instead of short periods of regular prison or jail confinement, when an offender needs the kinds of services the halfway house staff can provide.

Prison camps of various types, correctional institutions, prisons, and penitentiaries are used for the longer-term confinement of convicted offenders. Depending on the type of inmate, they can range in security from those with very few controls, to a very severely controlled environment where inmates are locked in cells most of the day. They usually are operated through a state corrections department headed by an administrator appointed by the governor. Federal prisons confine primarily offenders convicted of violating federal laws, and are operated by the Federal Bureau of Prisons, an agency of the U.S. Department of Justice.

Parole is a method of selectively releasing inmates from prison and providing them community supervision with a combination of certain reporting requirements, personal restrictions, and guidance. Parole usually operates through an appointed board or commission. The correctional institution's connection with the parole process is explained further in Chapter 14 of this manual.

*The relatively recent pattern of court intervention into the area of inmate rights has had an impact on the manner in which correctional programs and facilities are operated.*

## The Correctional Setting

Before the development of prisons in the United States during the late 1700s, corrections consisted of punishments ranging from verbal disapproval to public hanging, depending on the severity of the offense. Jails were used to house inmates before punishment, but there were no prisons or other long-term correctional facilities as we now know them. Prisons were established to carry out the courts' judgment for punishment. Using long-term confinement, rather than physical punishment, torture, or death, was viewed as a more humane means of satisfying society's need for punishment and crime prevention.

Early in American prison history, the element of "reform" was introduced. This is reflected in some of the early terminology—penitentiaries were established to provide inmates an opportunity to repent of their sins. Reformatories were created to provide vocational training and education, particularly for younger offenders. Later, rehabilitation and treatment became a part of the overall correctional vocabulary. This was based on the theory that offenders could be "cured" of criminal tendencies. This led to the introduction of

*Correctional administrators are seeking a more balanced view of corrections—one that attempts to provide for incapacitation, deterrence, retribution, and treatment.*

academic and vocational programs, psychological diagnosis, and other "treatment" programs, such as counseling and group therapy. This "medical model" borrowed heavily from the mental health field, but is no longer widely accepted as representing a practical reality.

In America of the late 1980s public sentiments against crime, the growth of drug abuse and related trafficking, and many other attitude changes are in the forefront of another series of shifts. The use of community programs is being recognized as necessary and effective, but it is difficult to find neighborhoods that are willing to have such programs near homes and schools. New technologies and new trends in labor management and human resources development challenge modern administrators in their day-to-day work. Scarce resources are finally being found for correctional construction, but the public has not grasped the long-term operational costs of these facilities.

Even so, today, correctional administrators are seeking a more balanced view of corrections—one that attempts to provide for:

- incapacitation (preventing a specific offender from committing more crimes while in prison),
- deterrence (setting an example with one offender that will prevent others from committing crimes),

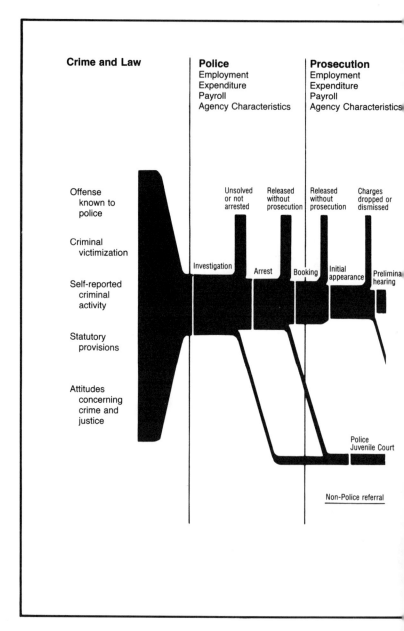

- retribution (punishment), and
- treatment (providing inmates who wish to change with the opportunity to do so).

This balance, while having positive effects, can also result in confusion for many as to the proper role of corrections and how its goals should be met. The challenge for each agency is to provide its staff with a clear view of the particular balance that its specific public, legal, and political setting demands.

## Court Intervention

The relatively recent pattern of court intervention into the area of inmate rights and institutional management has also had an impact on the manner in which correctional programs and facilities are operated. For many years, the courts had traditionally

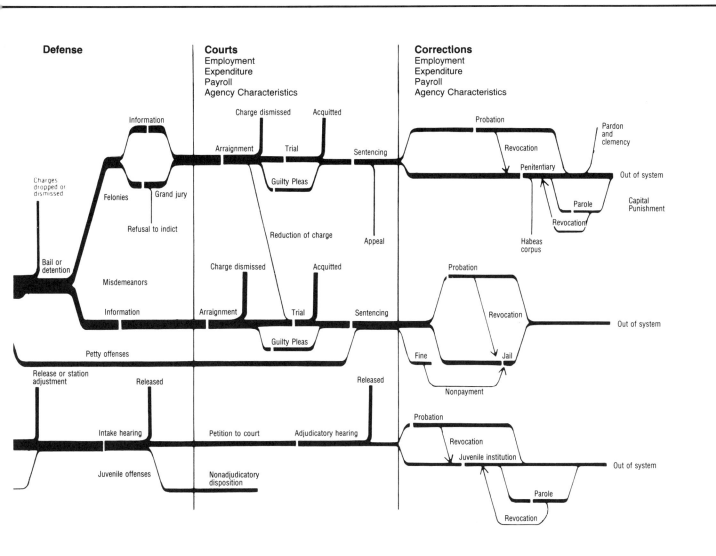

**Defense**

**Courts**
Employment
Expenditure
Payroll
Agency Characteristics

**Corrections**
Employment
Expenditure
Payroll
Agency Characteristics

Source: President's Commission on Law Enforcement and Administration of Justice, *The Challenge of Crime in a Free Society* (Washington, D.C.: U.S. Government Printing Office, 1967), pp. 8, 9.

taken a "hands-off" approach to corrections. The current concern for inmate rights was perhaps first seen in a 1944 court decision that ruled that "a prisoner retains all the rights of an ordinary citizen except those expressly, or by necessary implication taken by law." Court intervention began to occur more frequently after a 1971 court case that granted inmates access to the federal courts under the Civil Rights Act. Since then, a whole body of correctional caselaw has developed, affecting every phase of corrections. Entire state systems have been declared unconstitutional. Correctional administrators and officers have also been subject to civil suits, in which inmates claimed the employees were subject to paying damages personally, for their actions as prison employees.

As a result of this changing legal climate, prisons have had to make numerous changes. Some of them have resulted in abandoning long-standing policies

and procedures, in order to ensure the protection of inmates' individual rights. Others have included hiring many more staff, or providing significantly more resources to prison administrators to ensure unconstitutional conditions do not continue. Thus, the courts have made a tremendous impact on the correctional setting in recent years.

## Summary

Correctional officers play a key role in effective institutional operations, and it is necessary that they understand the criminal justice setting of which they are a part. This includes knowledge of the entire criminal justice system, as well as corrections' role as a component of that system.

# 2

# Officers' Responsibilities and Training

Corrections today is a varied, complex, difficult, and, at times, contradictory profession. Who should be locked up? Is imprisoning people humane? Are treatment programs effective? How do you decide who is released? These and many equally difficult questions are raised by the public, lawmakers, and others with an interest in crime and its causes and prevention.

After hundreds of years of American prison operations, the basic purpose of corrections is still being debated. One reason for this is that the public has changed its goals for corrections many times over the years. First the public wanted a simple alternative to torture and hanging, then it had a desire to reform offenders, followed by refinements in this treatment strategy. Now the public's priorities have shifted back to punishment of offenders and protection of the public.

In the midst of these changes, we train staff in methods they will use throughout their careers, build certain kinds of institutions that will last for decades, and develop specific management systems that last for many years. Somehow, these fixed quantities must adapt to changes in public feelings and our country's legal structure.

Indeed, correctional staff must still perform their duties, despite surges of public controversy, occasional hostility, and indifference on the part of most Americans regarding the penal system. This factor makes it hard for beginning correctional officers to understand exactly what their new career is all about.

One thing is certain—on a day-to-day basis, a correctional staff must manage its institution's security and inmate supervision in a competent and humane way because human lives depend on it. Outlining how that is done is the subject of this chapter, and indeed, the entire *Guide*.

## The Role of Corrections and Correctional Officers

Defining the role of the correctional officer actually starts with the mission of corrections. While different correctional organizations have quite different missions, for those with a confinement component, the one common factor is to carry out the courts' judgments and thereby protect the public by confining convicted offenders. Correctional staffs do not judge which offenders are so dangerous, violent, or troublesome as to require imprisonment. They don't decide what accountability or deterrence require in the way of a prison term for a specific offender. Corrections' first job is to accept the courts' judgment and confine inmates for the legal term of their sentences.

While other roles, such as providing treatment, clearly are also important, maintaining security is the first priority in any institution and the prime responsibility of correctional officers. Most of the other chapters in this publication tell how those prime responsibilities are carried out.

In many systems, there is an emphasis on the "correctional worker" concept, where every employee is a correctional officer first and a specialist in his or her field second. There is great merit to this approach, because it raises the security consciousness of all employees, and increases institutional security far more than if only the uniformed correctional force is involved. Indeed, a great deal of the information in this guide applies to everyone who works in an institution. But it is correctional officers who are most directly involved in maintaining security as a primary duty, and for that reason, these remarks are directed to them.

In addition to their primary security role,

correctional officers probably are the most important employees in inmates' lives. In most institutions, officers assign and supervise inmates as they eat, sleep, work, and exercise; control their movement; maintain security; and at times isolate or segregate those who are a threat to themselves or to others. Officers see inmates' subtle actions, reactions, and interactions—the slight behavior changes that can signal an inmate's personal problems, progress toward positive change, or an impending riot.

## Training

To carry out their security and supervision responsibilities, officers need to understand their agency's correctional philosophy and their institution's regulations and procedures. They must be security technicians—as expert in their search, supervision, and inmate management skills as a doctor is in surgery. They must know the limits of their responsibility and authority, as well as how to work as team members with other staffs, both correctional and noncorrectional. Finally, they must understand the judicial and legislative decisions that affect what they do. To know all of these important facts, a well-developed training program is necessary.

Poorly trained officers with no prior experience are a threat to themselves and to other staff. New officers without proper training have no idea of the proper role or job responsibilities of correctional officers. And yet most new correctional staff have no

*Maintaining security is the first priority in any institution and the prime responsibility of correctional officers.*

prior experience in working with inmates, and almost none have any training that applies to the prison setting.

That is why training is so critical. In fact, the American Correctional Association has established a standard that all new officers receive 40 hours of orientation and training before they receive independent assignment. At a minimum, this training can be used to familiarize new staff members with the purpose, goals, policies, and procedures of the institution and parent agency; working conditions and regulations; responsibilities; inmate rights; and an overview of the correctional field.

In many agencies, staff receive more training in line with ACA standards: an additional 120 hours of training during their first year of employment and 40 hours of training each following year. Courses typically cover the following information:

• Security procedures
• Supervision of inmates

- Use-of-force regulations and procedures
- Report writing
- Inmate rules and regulations
- Inmates' rights and responsibilities
- Fire and emergency procedures
- Firearms training
- Key control
- Interpersonal relations
- Social/cultural lifestyles of the inmate population
- Communication skills
- First aid

Training also has the potential to help staff members to:

- Advance in rank and salary
- Achieve personal development
- Develop ease in handling work assignments
- Develop sound judgment
- Acquire knowledge of occupational hazards
- Improve working conditions
- Increase dignity and pride in employment—develop a professional attitude
- Understand and practice the institution's philosophy and policies
- Improve job satisfaction

Specific skill training for correctional officers is often provided on an ongoing basis. Goals of such training include:

- To further improve the technical skills of correctional officers who must supervise inmates and implement the security program
- To increase the effectiveness of correctional officers and thereby obtain greater efficiency and economy in operations
- To provide correctional officers with the improved ability to recognize, understand, and solve the problems that occur in the correctional institution
- To offer correctional officers improved job satisfaction and career services

## Summary

The professional officer in today's correctional environment must have a wide variety of skills. A comprehensive, well-organized training program is essential to developing an effective work force. In addition to the institutional training program (which in many agencies is set up using ACA standards), correctional officers should also consider obtaining training from outside sources, such as community colleges, to improve their skills.

# 3

# Corrections and the Law

As part of their security responsibilities, correctional staff at every level are obligated to enforce and obey the law. They also must uphold the principles that the Constitution and federal courts set for correctional operations, including respecting the rights that inmates retain even while in custody. The Supreme Court has ruled that a prison regulation that infringes on inmates' constitutional rights is valid only "if it is reasonably related to legitimate penological interests." To respect those rights, a staff member needs to know what they are.

There is a possible legal consequence to virtually every aspect of correctional institutions, but knowing the legal issues that affect correctional operations will reduce the likelihood of litigation. Officers should perform as though their every action will be scrutinized at a later date. But at the same time, correctional staff who use good judgment, know policy, and have solid information to make their decisions will seldom, if ever, have serious legal problems.

## What Regulates an Institution's Operation?

Correctional agencies are operated in line with statutes, which are specific laws passed by the legislative body of that state or the federal government; by regulations issued by other government agencies, such as fire or safety codes; and by internal agency regulations or policies, set up by the agency itself to regulate its operations. In addition, the U.S. Constitution and state and federal court decisions on past lawsuits provide certain guidelines for correctional agencies, telling them how

they must act in specific areas such as inmate discipline and religious practices.

Staff members must be aware of the specific state and federal laws that regulate their actions and the operation of their institution. This information is most often given to employees through agency training programs, periodic retraining, and other internal agency communications such as newsletters.

Administrative regulations, which may be very complicated, fill in the details not covered by federal or state statutes. They are often quite specific, and it is important that officers clearly understand them, because they define how correctional officials can and should act in a given situation. Again, this information is often taught in specific institutional training programs and by other methods.

Agency policy is the most practical and flexible of these regulations, and usually gives the most useful information to staff members about how they are expected to do their jobs. In fact, policy is often very specific in each institution, and in many institutions employees can have some input into new policies and revision of existing policies.

The final category is the U.S. Constitution and the interpretation of laws that result from court decisions. The Constitution and its Amendments describe U.S. citizens' rights, many of which apply to inmates. Over the years, the courts have reviewed challenges to laws, actions, and decisions based on the claim they were not in line with the Constitution or its Amendments. As the number of these decisions grows, this body of caselaw, as it is called, is an important guiding factor for correctional personnel. Since the early 1970s, correctional law has changed rapidly. The courts have focused their attention on the correctional process and inmates' rights. As courts have reviewed a wide variety of cases during these years, the caselaw has grown, and so has the need for correctional staff to be more aware of the legal consequences of their actions.

## Why Might an Officer Be Sued by an Inmate?

Inmates often file lawsuits against staff, either as individuals or as part of the agency structure, because they honestly believe their rights have been violated. In other cases, suits are filed as harassment, or in an attempt to intimidate staff or prevent them from doing their jobs. In either case, a lawsuit filed by an inmate is a serious matter, and staff should not take it lightly.

*Whether a staff member is liable for some injury to an inmate frequently depends on whether the officer's conduct involved a failure to fulfill the duty to protect.*

It is a well-accepted principle of law that correctional staff have a duty to protect inmates, within certain limits. Whether a staff member is liable for some injury to an inmate frequently depends on whether the officer's conduct involved a failure to fulfill this duty to protect. Courts use a "reasonableness" test to determine if correctional staff have acted unreasonably in performing their duties. By that, it is meant that courts will review the facts of a case, and try to decide if the actions taken by the staff member were those that a reasonable person would have taken under the same circumstances. For instance, staff have been sued for failure to protect an inmate who had been stabbed, and have been found not liable, as long as some logical procedures were in place and they were followed in a reasonable way. The duty to protect is not absolute, but it is an important one nevertheless.

Other lawsuits can hinge on the difference between "what is done" and "how it is done." For example, under some circumstances, an inmate may be able to challenge the right of a correctional officer to place an inmate in segregation, by alleging either that the act itself was unconstitutional (maybe for no good reason), or that the way it was done (perhaps without a hearing) was unconstitutional. In other words, some acts are illegal no matter how they are done, and others are illegal if they are not carried out according to the law.

Inmates can ask a judge to consider their individual complaint, or they can sue in a class action. That is a type of group case on behalf of all the inmates who have similar complaints or who are similarly situated (such as all inmates in a segregation unit), even though it may not be immediately provable that all have the same problem.

Depending on the nature of the complaint, an inmate can sue either the state, the correctional agency, the head of the agency, or the particular officer who allegedly caused the injury or deprived the inmate of the specific constitutional right. Fortunately, most inmates do not file lawsuits directly against line officers. Instead, they challenge rules and policies established by administrators or other officials. While it is the responsibility of a supervising officer to know policy and give appropriate, legal orders to subordinates, the courts have said in some circumstances that if a reasonable person should have known of the right involved, the subordinates can be liable.

The possibility of a staff member being held personally liable to pay an inmate, or inmates, financial damages is very real in some instances. This concept of personal liability is important. The

# Helpful Legal Definitions

The legal profession often uses terms that are unusual, or uses common terms in a specific and different way. The following basic legal definitions should prove helpful to correctional officers.

*Administrative Remedy*—a first-level attempt to solve a problem through internal agency procedures, used before a lawsuit is filed

*Affidavit*—a sworn statement filed by an individual in which he or she states under oath that, to his or her personal knowledge, an event or series of events occurred

*Appeal*—a formal process for having a higher authority or higher court review a decision. In the U.S. legal system, the Supreme Court can review and overturn decisions of all other courts—state and federal—thus making its rulings the "law of the land"

*Attorneys' Fees*—fees awarded to the lawyer who represents a successful plaintiff in a civil rights action. These are awarded independently of and in addition to any award in favor of the plaintiff and can be considerably larger than whatever the plaintiff receives

*Case*—the general term used to refer to a lawsuit, or even criminal proceedings, that an inmate is involved in

*Caselaw*—the collected body of court decisions on a particular subject that guides administrators in their actions and policies

*Civil*—portions of the law that relate to noncriminal activity, that is, actions that generally involve the private rights of citizens

*Complaint*—the formal name for a legal document filed by an inmate with a court, alleging some violation of rights or statute; usually when personal liability is involved, a copy of the complaint must be served personally on the defendant

*Court Cap*—the limit sometimes placed on prison populations by a court when prison populations exceed constitutional limits, in the eyes of the court

*Court Monitor*—a person, often a lawyer, appointed by a court to monitor compliance with a court's order entered after some aspect or aspects of a prison's operation has been found to be unconstitutional

*Criminal*—activity relating to acts that are defined by law as crimes

*Defendant*—the person sued in a lawsuit

*Deposition*—another type of sworn statement, usually given by someone involved in a lawsuit, which is taken in the company of attorneys from both sides, and recorded by a court reporter

*Immunity*—the legal protection sometimes available to staff that means they are not subject to a judgment for their official acts; there are several types of immunity that apply in different situations

*Judgment*—a court ruling on a case, which in a civil matter may involve some type of order to remedy an improper condition or an order for a defendant to pay costs or money damages; in a criminal case the defendant may be required to serve a sentence of some type

*Lawsuit*—a term used to refer to the formal process of an inmate suing a staff member or the institution

*Liability*—the term used for legal responsibility or guilt for an improper act taken by a defendant

*Litigation*—the general term for court activity relating to a lawsuit

*Plaintiff*—the person suing in a lawsuit

*Served*—a term for formally giving a legal document to a person involved in a suit

*Special Master*—another type of outside party who may be used by the court to oversee prison operations if they have been found to be unconstitutional

*Statute*—another name for a law

*Subpoena*—an order for a person to appear for some type of formal legal process, such as a trial

*Suit*—another name for lawsuit

*Summons*—another type of document that tells a person he or she is part of a legal action

*(ACA Legal Issues Committee, 1989)*

Supreme Court has said that officials may not be held liable if they did not violate constitutional or statutory rights, clearly established at the time of the offense, of which a reasonable person would have known.

All agencies provide legal support to their staff who are sued in the course of their official duties. It is the responsibility of the staff member to immediately inform the agency when he or she is served with a copy of a complaint, summons, or subpoena. Virtually all state agencies have a policy that states that they will reimburse an employee for adverse court judgments resulting from official duties in certain, but not all, cases. It is rare for agencies to refuse to defend suits brought against employees and/or refuse to pay all costs associated with those suits.

## Federal Constitutional Lawsuits

Most inmate cases involve federal constitutional rights. Inmates most often sue based on the following provisions of the federal Constitution:

• *First Amendment.* The First Amendment provides for freedom of religion, speech, and the press. The Supreme Court has ruled that inmates have only those First Amendment rights that are consistent with prison discipline and do not conflict with the legitimate penological objectives of institutional administration. Inmates most often claim violations of

*There is a possible legal consequence to virtually every aspect of correctional institutions . . . Officers should perform as though their every action will be scrutinized at a later date.*

## Most inmates do not file lawsuits directly against line officers. Instead, they challenge rules and policies established by administrators or other officials.

this Amendment when they believe their right to exercise their personal religious beliefs has been improperly restricted. For example, courts have ruled it is improper to force a Muslim to handle or eat pork, because of the prohibition of the Islamic religion against contact with pork or pork products.

Correspondence is another area of concern, often because of staff decisions to censor or reject correspondence and publications sent to inmates. In these cases, the courts are concerned both with the reasons for censorship and the procedures followed in making the censorship decision. The key principle in all of these cases is to be in line with legitimate penological objectives of the institution's administration, such as the need to prevent inmates from receiving contraband through the mails, or to stop escape-related information from coming into the institution.

• *Fourth Amendment.* This Amendment prohibits "unreasonable" searches and seizures. The extent to which inmates and their property can be searched is the subject of frequent litigation under the Fourth Amendment. For example, a common question is whether a particular type of search (patdown, strip search, probe, or body cavity search) may be done randomly, or whether there must be some "cause" to justify the search. Ordinarily, agency policy will guide staff on an issue like this, but an inmate may challenge whether or not a specific reason was sufficient to justify a specific search. It is important to remember that an inmate may also sue under the Fourth Amendment when correctional searches are performed unprofessionally, in ways that unnecessarily humiliate the inmate. The key issues in cases of this type are whether the staff member had a reasonable basis for conducting the search, and whether it was carried out within policy.

• *Eighth Amendment.* This Amendment prohibits cruel and unusual punishment. Cases filed under this category usually deal with prison conditions in general. Individual acts of mistreatment (such as beating an inmate) may be, of themselves, cruel and unusual punishment. However, courts most often consider the overall conditions of an institution—in

other words, they determine whether a facility is adequately providing for basic human needs. In recent years, the courts have been very firm in requiring agencies and institutions to correct conditions of confinement that are not consistent with the changing standards of decency in society. In other words, just because bad food, unsanitary conditions, and no programs were acceptable 25 years ago, does not mean that the courts will approve them now; society expects more from its prisons now, and correctional staff must live up to those expectations.

• *Fourteenth Amendment.* This Amendment prohibits the taking of life, liberty, or property without due process of law. This type of case is ordinarily directed at the way correctional staff restrict inmates, or take their property. There are certain kinds of freedom that cannot be taken from an inmate (even in the institution) without having a hearing or other formal procedure. Giving some kind of formal review of this type, under specific rules, is called providing due process. For instance, inmate property cannot be taken away permanently, or an inmate placed in disciplinary status, without due process. Agency policy will spell out the conditions under which these hearings are required, and how they are to be conducted. The decision-making process must be fair and the results of the decision must be fairly applied.

16

The Fourteenth Amendment also requires equal protection under the law; it prohibits different treatment of two individuals who are in similar circumstances, without proper justification. As an example, correctional policies that unjustifiably treat inmates differently on the basis of religion or race are unconstitutional. Recent Fourteenth Amendment cases have also stated that male and female inmates must be treated equivalently (though not identically) with respect to conditions of their confinement and their access to programs. Agencies have been ordered to upgrade the educational and vocational programs offered in female institutions so that they would be equivalent to programs offered in male institutions.

Finally, some Fourteenth Amendment cases are brought because inmates allege inadequate access to the courts. These are often a result of a correctional officer removing legal materials from an inmate's property, restricting access to the law library, or some other similar problem. These cases often can be avoided by being thoroughly familiar with the rules of the institution regarding inmate access to these legal resources. Retaliation by an officer against an inmate for filing a suit (even if the suit turns out to have no merit) will be seen as a violation of the inmate's right of access to the court.

## Other Circumstances for Lawsuits

In addition to possible constitutional grounds for a suit, cases can be filed on the basis of an allegation of a violation of law. The Civil Rights Act of 1871 is frequently used by state inmates who believe their federal constitutional rights have been violated. Correctional officers must be aware that under this law, inmates can sue for alleged violations of constitutional rights by staff who improperly use their authority under state law. This law also permits inmates, in appropriate cases, to receive financial damages from those convicted of violating these rights.

Fortunately, the courts do not find a significant percentage of inmate lawsuits brought under this Act, as a result of prison-related injuries, to be constitutional abuse. For example, a lawsuit filed by an inmate injured during a scuffle with a correctional officer probably will not succeed unless the facts showed that in the aftermath, for instance, the officer continued to strike the inmate long after the situation was under control. In another example, an inmate claiming improper medical care must be able to prove that there was deliberate indifference to the alleged illness or injury; mere medical malpractice does not amount to a constitutional violation in such circumstances. Cases where the inmate succeeds in a lawsuit often involve an assault or other incident that was so violent, unprovoked, or dramatic as to either shock the court's conscience or violate basic fairness.

Staff members should be aware that when a federal case cannot be filed successfully, the actions of correctional officials in the above examples still may give the inmates grounds for a nonfederal lawsuit based on other legal theories, such as tort claims. Those actions usually must be initiated in the state courts, and the grounds for those cases vary from state to state.

It is also important to note that in extreme cases, correctional staff have been prosecuted under criminal laws for their actions in the correctional setting. Violating an inmate's civil rights is a federal offense, and while fortunately rare, there are occasional instances when prison staff members actually have served federal criminal sentences for their improper acts.

## Inmate Access to Legal Resources

Many new correctional employees have difficulty understanding that inmates still retain certain rights while in prison. And one of the most important, and difficult to accept, is that they have a right to access the courts. It is a clearly accepted fact of correctional life that inmates must be given access to legal resources. It is just as clear that improperly restricting that access is highly illegal.

These legal resources typically include a law library in the institution, permission to keep personal legal materials in their cells, the ability to mail uncensored letters to and from their attorneys, the right to unmonitored telephone calls to attorneys, and the right to private visits with attorneys. Even inmates in segregation have a right to these activities, although they may be somewhat modified in the interest of institutional security.

Every state and federal jurisdiction has somewhat different rules on this issue, so it is not possible to go into any great detail in this publication. Every agency has an obligation to make these requirements known to its staff, and every staff member has an important obligation to permit inmates proper access to these resources.

## Reducing Litigation

Every dispute between inmates and staff does not have to result in a lawsuit—clearly, not all do or the courts would be totally jammed with prison cases. In addition to common-sense relations with inmates that reduce conflict, one well-established method many agencies use to reduce litigation is an administrative remedy process or other internal grievance procedure. Many courts have decided that before an individual can ask to have a case heard in court, all possible non-court options, or administrative remedies, should have been tried. For that reason, many correctional agencies have set up grievance or administrative remedy systems to try to resolve inmate complaints before they reach the court.

In a properly administered grievance system, the inmate's formal, written complaint will be reviewed and investigated at the institution by a person who was not involved in the original decision. In some systems, there are even regional office and headquarters office appeals possible. At every level, the inmate will receive a formal, written response to the grievance.

Some inmates don't like to use these systems, because they slow down the process of filing a lawsuit. Others see the value of getting results without having to go to court. In any case, staff members who are doing their job properly have nothing to fear from inmates filing a grievance against them. These informal methods of adjusting problems are good management. Just as importantly, where a formal system is in place, staff must not prevent an inmate from using that system, because to do so may mean that a potentially solvable problem may then move directly to court.

## The Importance of Report Writing

It is very likely that any review, whether by administrative remedy or a court, will happen long after the event. That means a report should be written whenever an unusual incident occurs. Clear, concise, factual reporting of an incident is important to the reviewer in the event of an outside review.

Correctional officers are often the first staff involved in incidents that lead to lawsuits in an institution. As a result, their actions often determine the outcome of later reviews, and reports should be filed at the time of events, while memory of the incident is still fresh. These reports may be reviewed at internal disciplinary hearings, as part of the grievance process, or introduced in court proceedings. An accurate report will also improve the officer's ability to testify factually if a particular case should ever result in a trial.

Any report must contain information on "who, what, where, when, why, and how." For instance, a report stating only that an inmate was locked up as a "threat to the security of the institution," without detailing the threat, tells the reader very little. It certainly would be no help in refreshing a staff member's memory several years later if the matter ever went to court.

## Summary

Correctional law is constantly changing, particularly in the last 20 years. As corrections achieves an even more professional place in American society, its administrative rules will further reflect a clearer sense of purpose, new staff awareness of legal matters, and a broader view of inmate rights. Correctional officers who understand the importance of legal issues will be far more effective in their daily work, and will be better equipped to progress in their careers.

The information in this section provides only an overview of correctional training and applicable law; staff are encouraged to obtain additional information specific to their agency, and to keep current on procedures, and, through staff training, remain up-to-date on court decisions affecting their job.

*APPLICABLE ACA STANDARDS*

Inmates' Rights: 3-4262 to 3-4271, 3-4387, and 3-4395

# 4

# Inmate Supervision and Discipline

orrectional officers are key figures in managing a well-run institution. To be effective, they must have a command of policies and procedures, know and effectively use the many security and supervision techniques employed in modern prisons, and at the same time treat inmates in a fair, humane way.

Supervision is more than simply visual observation; line staff and supervisors must be actively involved in every aspect of the facility's operation. They must actively control inmates and their activities every moment of the day. This involves issuing orders, performing counts, working towers, mastering surveillance technology, maintaining personal contact with inmates, and much more. Although it seems inconsistent at first, supervising inmates inside the facility is actually the key to perimeter security, because if inmates are not adequately controlled inside the perimeter, they will eventually be able to find ways to escape, no matter how secure the institution.

## Interacting with Inmates

The degree of supervision required by inmates varies according to their classification. The principles behind classification are discussed in later chapters in this guide, but generally speaking, inmates with similar security and supervision needs are housed in the same institution.

A good classification system provides for a regular review of inmates' cases, so that staff can move those who need more or less security to the proper location. As a rule, as inmates move closer to the end of their sentences, they can be moved to lower security settings. However, every system always has a few

high-security inmates whose custody or supervision level should not be reduced at any point in their sentences.

Corrections is a very intense people business. In starting their career, correctional officers, and indeed every correctional worker, would do well to assess their attitudes toward others, and particularly toward inmates as human beings. Many people, because of their negative attitudes, cannot work with any degree of success in an institution. Without the proper attitude, it is almost impossible to do a good job for the institution, or to deal effectively with inmates. If an officer does not have some degree of personal concern about inmates as human beings, then no amount of training, education, or supervision will make it possible to effectively supervise and assist them.

### Impartial Rule Enforcement

However, it is important that officers not let their personal beliefs and feelings affect their interactions with inmates. Impartial rule enforcement is the best way to gain inmates' ready compliance. Officers can get more cooperation if they convey their authority through fair actions and neutral attitudes, rather than through overbearing, heavy-handed tactics.

Given that every inmate is a unique person, it stands to reason that inmates will respond differently to the same treatment. However, fair, impartial treatment is one of the cornerstones of prison life; inequality is almost certain to create serious problems. Some decisions can and should be individualized, and the circumstances where that is appropriate are often spelled out in policy. In other instances, what to do is not immediately clear. Sometimes experience is the best teacher; a new officer should rely on more experienced staff and supervisors for advice in questionable instances.

## Direct Versus Indirect Supervision

New institutional designs have greatly improved officers' ability to directly supervise inmates. Smaller housing units, interior layouts that provide easy visibility into all parts of the unit, and other design features all make it easier for an officer to maintain contact with inmates, and thus know what is going on in the unit. This type of design reflects a personal staff contact philosophy; employees interact with inmates, move freely throughout the unit and shakedown rooms, and are generally personally involved in unit operations.

However, some designs in recent years have moved in the direction of less staff contact with inmates, instead of more. Units with a remote supervision design are often characterized by electromechanically operated doors activated by a unit control center, where the assigned officer stays locked in all day, having very little contact with the inmates in the unit. Housing areas with these designs are sometimes staffed with an officer "on the floor" also, but when they do, they have the management drawback of requiring twice as many employees for the same size inmate population. The advantage of these designs is said to be in the area of staff safety. The disadvantages stem from employees having far less normal interaction with inmates; staff search inmates and their cells less often, and generally know less about what is going on in the unit.

There has been considerable debate in recent years about the relative merits of these two design philosophies. To the degree that it favors normal interaction with inmates and more direct supervision and search activity, direct supervision designs are felt to be more advantageous in most institutions. For those few units, and even fewer total institutions, where ultrahigh security needs may dictate a unit control center, the indirect contact strategy may have merit. But even in those locations, staff must still be in contact with inmates, if only for conducting searches, applying restraints, and performing other direct contact functions. In short, an inmate housing unit must be supervised through direct, hands-on techniques if it is to remain secure and safe.

## Issuing Orders

Officers often must make inmates do things they do not want to do, and inmate reactions to orders are sometimes threatening. As difficult as it may be when confronted by hostile or defiant inmates, correctional officers must maintain self-control and a professional attitude, while insisting on compliance. If the inmate cannot be persuaded to comply with an order, then assistance should be called.

*No matter how secure the perimeter, if the interior of an institution is improperly supervised, eventually the inmates will find a way to breach the security.*

To successfully give orders and instructions, avoid vague or inappropriate words, confusing instructions, or incomplete information. If an officer permits the inmate to not follow an order, then one of the basic elements of control in the institution begins to break down. Refusing an order can be direct, in which case it can be dealt with directly. In other cases, it may instead be through passive or obstructive activity, in which the inmate works slowly or in a way that actually sabotages the job. Officers must intervene in those instances also.

Some inmates may be legitimately unable to comply with an order on a matter that is essentially discretionary. Officers need to be flexible and especially alert to medical or mental health problems that can prevent a specific inmate from doing something. In medical cases, the medical staff may issue special orders, such as one for a lower bunk, a bed board, a "fifth feeding" meal, or some other variation of normal operations. One may ask, "Well, isn't that treating inmates unequally—isn't that unfair?" Yes, it is treating them unequally, but it is

## Signs of Trouble

Certain inmate behaviors may be a sign of impending trouble—the tension that precedes a riot, for instance. Disturbances can be prevented if staff observe, and report, changes in the following routines:

- Separation by racial or ethnic groups
- Purchases of foodstuffs at inmate canteens
- Transfer requests
- Staff requests for sick leave
- Inmate cell time
- Inmate groupings with point men facing away from the group
- Numbers of disciplinary cases
- Numbers of voluntary lockups
- Inmate/employee confrontations
- Direct and indirect inmate intimidation of officers
- Threats against officers
- Inmate sick calls
- Inmate violence against other inmates
- Number of weapons found in shakedowns
- Harsh stares from inmates
- Drop in attendance at movies or other popular functions
- Unusual and/or subdued actions by inmate groups
- Reluctance on the part of inmates to communicate with staff
- Inmates avoiding eye contact with staff
- Inmates making excessive and/or specific demands
- Appearance of inflammatory and rebellious materials
- Warnings to "friendly" officers to take sick leave or vacation
- Employee demands for safety
- Staff resignations
- Letters and/or phone calls from concerned inmate families demanding protection for inmates
- Unusual number of telephone inquiries about prison conditions
- Outside agitation by lawyers or activists

not unfair. In optional or judgment call areas, other inmates will understand an officer granting a variation in a routine order if there is a legitimate reason, and as long as it does not violate basic institutional procedures or security.

## Observing Inmates

Individual and group activities, and the patterns and habits they represent, can be important indicators of an institution's mood or of illegal activity. Staff observation practices should include not only obvious duties like breaking up fights and searching inmates and their cells, but also awareness of the subtle day-to-day changes in an institution, a unit, or individual inmates.

When an inmate who has previously been sullen and secretive begins to act friendly and cooperative, officers should be suspicious, and investigate immediately, reporting the change to a supervisor. Inmates who are anxious, who withdraw from group activities, who become careless about their personal appearance, or show other clear behavior changes are also a concern. However, changes in an inmate's behavior are not necessarily negative, and making judgments on which changes are a cause for concern becomes easier with time and experience.

## Supervision in Housing Units

Consistent supervision is essential for the safe and orderly operation of any correctional institution, and there is perhaps no place where that is more true than in the housing unit. An officer's poor judgment, lack of consistency, favoritism, or undue severity can change a quiet, peaceful housing unit into a dangerous place.

Officers' observation of inmate behavior in the housing area can lead to the discovery of escape plots, contraband, and other serious security concerns. Security inspections and routine but unpredictable shakedowns of cells and common areas are critical to this process. Observing changes in behavior, attitude, friends, and other factors can also be important. These changes may signal an inmate under pressure for sex, one who has just started using drugs, an escape plot in the works, or any number of other problems.

Enforcing daily routines is very important in the smooth management of the housing area. These routines include wakeup, cell cleaning, cleaning of common areas, enforcement of noise-level restrictions and personal property limits, and many others. They also ordinarily include enforcing rules restricting inmate visits from other housing units, searches of incoming inmates, searches of all materials, carts, tool boxes, and other items moving into the unit, and general traffic control.

During the day, most inmates are released from their cell blocks or dormitories to go to work or programs. While responsible for the general accountability of the remaining inmates, the housing unit officer is also responsible for supervising inmates who clean and maintain the unit. This may be on a rotating basis, but a fixed set of tasks should be accomplished on a regular schedule. Standards for what constitutes properly completed work must not vary from day to day, and staff should remember that inmates will never do a better job than staff insist they do. If low standards are acceptable, the institution will deteriorate. Jobs should be organized in correct operational sequence; cleaning materials and equipment must be properly used and stored at the conclusion of work.

Correctional officers should inspect for signs of unsafe or deteriorating facilities, i.e., cracked paint, broken windows, and faulty plumbing, as well as evidence of tampered bars and locking devices, which could result in escape or injury either to inmates or to employees. These sanitation, maintenance, and security inspections are very important for keeping the institution running in a safe, secure fashion.

## Post Orders, Logs, and Records

Unit logs should be maintained, reflecting events on every shift. They should include inmate transfers in and out, major maintenance or security issues and to whom they have been reported, and any details or concerns regarding the group as a whole or individual inmates in particular. These records are important for maintaining continuity from shift to shift.

Each unit should have a set of post orders describing the major duties of the post on a chronological basis, as well as certain topical information. In addition, post orders typically have sections with portions of major policies that affect the post's operation. These might include, for instance, placing sections of the hostage or use-of-force policies in the post orders of a high-security unit, or portions of the inmate accountability policy in the post orders of all housing units.

Bed books, picture cards, and other inmate records, including basic sentence information, should be maintained in the unit, to enable staff to correctly and quickly identify every inmate in the unit and their living areas, whether cells or dormitory bunks. A picture card system enables staff to quickly determine who may be missing in an escape attempt or other major problem.

## Information Issues

Reliable information, systematically collected and analyzed, helps in regularly supervising and managing the institution, and can prevent riots or other disturbances. Collecting intelligence data is a daily operation and includes receiving input from all personnel. Information gathered by supervisory,

*Staff observation practices should include not only obvious duties like breaking up fights and searching inmates and their cells, but also awareness of the subtle day-to-day changes in an institution, a unit, or individual inmates.*

commissary, medical, program, and line staff is channeled to one place, usually an investigative supervisor. That employee analyzes the information, determines its significance, and briefs top staff about the inmate population's mood and other important information.

To gather this information, sound relationships must be maintained with inmates so they are willing to communicate their problems and concerns. This is where the contact supervision strategy is valuable, because if staff are regularly interacting with inmates, this information will almost naturally flow to them.

If used responsibly and with proper verification, inmates are good sources of information. To a great degree, this is because most of them want to do their time without problems, and in a well-managed, safe institution. Riots, escapes, and other disruptions in the facility's routine may result in lost visits, reduced industrial wages, and other lost privileges, and may put the inmates at physical risk. So most inmates have an interest in seeing that the institution runs smoothly, and will often see that staff know in advance about impending problems—so long as the channels of communication are open and natural, as they are in an institution where staff are visible, active, and involved. On the other hand, inmates who serve as regular informants with personal gain as a motive are not only despised by other inmates but using them extensively can be disastrous. During the 1980 riot in Santa Fe, N.M., numerous informants were murdered by fellow inmates.

Information is a two-way street, however, and both inmates and staff must receive official information about programs and policies, particularly when changes are to be made or new policies instituted. Post orders—instructions about various job duties and policies—should be on all posts throughout the institution, for regular review by staff and supervisors. Staff bulletin boards, roll calls, institution newsletters, and other communication devices are also important.

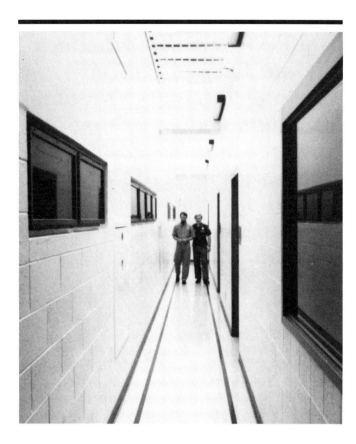

To prevent dangerous gaps in communication, officers should brief each other during shift changes. The relieving officer should be made aware of the current situation when coming on duty. The personal information passed on from one officer to another is supplemented by carefully kept unit logs and other records on post.

Likewise, inmates should be kept up-to-date on facts. When they lack good information from reliable staff sources, rumors and misinformation spread throughout the institution, which can lead to unrest and disorder. Newsletters, bulletin boards, and unit meetings can be good means to provide this information to the population.

## Supervising Inmates at Work

Correctional officers are often involved in supervising inmates on job assignments such as the kitchen, shops, and farm and camp details. These duties, of course, vary from job to job, but the following principles apply in almost all cases.

• A callout sheet of some type is commonly used to identify the time and place of authorized inmate appointments out of the unit or off the job, such as to food service, counseling, or medical appointments.

• All inmates on the detail should be accounted for at the beginning and end of the work period by use of a work detail picture card system; they must be required to stay in the authorized work area.

• During the day, periodic census checks or informal counts can help ensure proper accountability.

• Using an internal pass system can be a great aid in controlling inmate movement from jobs to programs, or other areas as needed, and after regular business hours for special groups or programs.

• Inmates and their work areas should be periodically but irregularly searched.

• Inmates using tools should be carefully supervised to ensure they are not using them in an unsafe manner or for manufacturing contraband or weapons.

• No inmate or group of inmates should be allowed to control other inmates; only correctional staff are legally authorized to supervise inmates.

## General Surveillance

Control centers facilitate surveillance by providing a totally secure location where staff can observe inmate movement and activity, control gates and grilles, monitor security equipment, and generally direct institutional operations. Monitors for closed-circuit televisions are used to control traffic and supervise key inmate movements. Control centers are, indeed, the nerve center of most institutions.

Towers are another important supervision element in institutions that have them. Tower officers are in a position to not only supervise the perimeter itself, but to watch for unusual inmate activity inside and outside the compound. The use of high-powered binoculars from towers can even be a factor in supervising inmate activity in cells and certain areas of the institution where visibility through windows makes it possible to see inside a building or into a courtyard.

Perimeter patrols can have a similar function, although their ground-level position of observing through a fence places them at a disadvantage in detecting unusual activity inside the compound. Nevertheless, outside patrols can detect unusual activity on the part of inmates working on outside work details, or by visitors. They certainly can be a deterrent to the introduction of contraband over fences or walls, or to civilians "stashing" contraband in nearby locations for later pickup by outside inmate workers.

Electronic surveillance systems are increasingly important in extending staff resources in the day-to-day supervision of institutions. These typically include closed-circuit television, motion detection devices, metal detection equipment, and electronic fence alarm systems based on microwave, vibration, or other technologies. These devices must be viewed as aids to supervision, not replacements for human intervention.

While they may be excellent in detecting activity in unauthorized areas, or in alerting staff to unusual groupings of inmates, if not used properly or monitored properly, they can produce a false sense of security. It is not possible to blanket an institution with enough television cameras, sound systems, and metal detectors to stop all contraband traffic and escape attempts. The best security will always be staff-inmate contacts and the personal actions of staff in searching inmates, their cells, and common areas.

## Inmate Transportation

Each institution or agency has its own regulations on the transportation of inmates. This guide will not attempt to describe all of the possible situations that may be encountered, from court trips to supervision of medical cases. However, the following are a few common factors in most trips that should be noted.

• Every inmate leaving the institution must be properly identified, and the releasing documents properly authenticated. Whenever possible, staff escorting an inmate outside the institution should have an opportunity to review the inmate's file to

learn any relevant background information, such as a history of escapes or assaults.

• When possible, inmates leaving on escorted trips should be searched by the escorting staff; it is not wise to trust another employee's search of an inmate when personal safety is at stake.

• Restraints should be carefully inspected before applying them, and regularly reinspected while on the inmate to detect any signs of tampering.

• Inmates under escort should never be permitted to come in direct contact with an armed staff member.

• Inmates should not be permitted to come into contact with the public.

## Sexual Behavior in the Correctional Setting

Inmate sexual activity is a particularly important supervision issue, even though it is not permitted in the correctional setting, except for a few family visiting programs. Many inmates are sexually preoccupied as a direct result of their deprivation of heterosexual relationships. Many are young adults, and their sexual drive is an extremely strong factor in their behavior. Staff need to understand this aspect of inmate behavior and prepare themselves to deal with it appropriately.

The lack of heterosexual relations can cause different types of behavior. Masturbation is certainly not unusual in the correctional setting. To the extent allowed by institution regulations, there may be pinups, photos, and written material that have sexual overtones. Also, staff members of the opposite sex receive a great deal of attention; this attention may be in the form of direct or indirect propositions or sexual comments.

## Heterosexual Activity

Heterosexual activity is a problem in those few institutions where male and female inmates are confined in the same location, or when staff members of the opposite gender of the population are involved.

Staff must be careful to provide the highest possible level of supervision to inmates in institutions where both sexes are confined. Supervision of mixed groups, and of areas where inmates might hide, are major issues. The potential problems associated with these programs are often said to be offset by the improved atmosphere of the institution, and the less dehumanized environment. However, there has not been any great movement in recent years toward establishing many of these co-correctional institutions.

It should go without saying that staff-inmate sexual activity is completely forbidden in all institutions. Yet with the assignment of staff of both genders to institutions housing the opposite sex, this is a problem from time to time.

No staff member should initiate, or allow to start, any personal or intimate relationship with an inmate. In addition to individual staff members being totally professional in their interactions with inmates and alert to any overtures that may signal an inmate trying to start an intimate relationship, supervisory staff must be constantly alert for the signs of any unusually close relationship between an inmate and a staff member. Staff who receive overtures from an inmate should report them to supervisory personnel at once, as a safeguard against later allegations of improper conduct that might be made by the inmate.

## Homosexual Activity

Correctional officers should be prepared to encounter homosexual behavior among inmates in the correctional setting. It is not surprising that homosexual contacts occur in prison, because it is a single-sex environment. Because of this abnormal setting, and because sex drives are likely to continue regardless of the environment, it is not uncommon for an otherwise heterosexual inmate to be involved in homosexual activities while in prison. Many of these inmates return to a heterosexual lifestyle once released to the community.

Some passive-partner male homosexuals play the female role in sexual activity, but do not adopt any female behavior; in their outward appearance, they may act rough and talk tough, but they can be identified by the company they keep. Others act in a directly feminine way, and if permitted to do so, may use make-up, swing their hips, wear feminine clothes, and generally act in a way to attract male attention.

Aggressive males involved in homosexual activity often act as "wolves" and prey on weaker or newer inmates to get sexual partners. These individuals should be watched carefully because of the trouble they can cause through their predatory sexual activity.

In male prisons, homosexuality can cause a great many problems. Sexual activity in a male institution not only reflects the sex drive, but also represents power or dominance. Competition, rivalries, and death can result from homosexual relationships that are allowed to develop or continue. For this reason, they represent not only a threat to the participants, but also to the institution's overall security.

*No staff member should initiate, or allow to start, any personal or intimate relationship with an inmate.*

In female institutions, sexual activity can have less of the aggressive or power overtones of a male institution. Inmates do adopt "male" roles, and some dress and act the part. However, there is also a "family" context that sometimes emerges as well, which is thought to satisfy the different emotional needs that female inmates have.

Homosexual affairs in prisons or jails are no joke, and should not be treated as such. Overt, weak homosexuals should be properly supervised and may need protection from "wolves." Some prisons and jails require that known homosexuals be kept under strict surveillance; some place them in isolation. On the other hand, homosexuals should not be ridiculed or unnecessarily singled out for special treatment; they are entitled to the same fair, professional treatment that any other inmate would receive.

To decrease homosexual activity, correctional officers must closely supervise inmates. This includes making sure inmates are in their assigned areas, supervising shower and bathing areas, encouraging inmate participation in recreational activities as an outlet for their energy, and not allowing the view into cells to be blocked by blankets, towels, sheets, or other objects.

When an inmate indicates a sexual assault has taken place, staff should act immediately. Supervisory personnel should be notified, and a decision made whether to place the victim in locked status or protective custody. The victim should be interviewed to identify the person or persons who committed the assault. In some cases, criminal prosecution may be indicated for the attackers, in addition to internal inmate discipline procedures. The victim should be referred for a medical examination and any appropriate medical care. A referral to mental health staff may also be indicated, as the trauma following such an event may lead to serious psychological problems.

Finally, there is the less common possibility of an inmate making a homosexual overture to a staff member. Just as in the case of sexual activity between opposite sexes, this is forbidden, and should be reported to supervisory staff at once.

## Disciplinary Procedures

Every correctional institution has rules to ensure good work performance, high sanitation and safety levels, and, most importantly, institutional security. These rules, if properly enforced, result in an orderly and acceptable way of life in the prison; they are especially necessary when large numbers of people live and work together.

If rules are disobeyed in prison, some form of punishment must be imposed. This punishment can range from a verbal reprimand to disciplinary status in a locked unit, from loss of good time to prosecution for a new offense committed in the institution.

Understandably, discipline and punishment are as unpopular within a correctional facility as they are in any other type of community. But discipline is most effectively imposed when inmates believe the process is fair. Well-defined rules of conduct, along with firm, fairly administered but not overly severe penalties, are critical to any disciplinary program.

ACA standards require each institution to provide inmates with a rule book that contains all chargeable offenses, ranges of penalties, and a description of disciplinary procedures. The rule book should be available in the languages spoken by significant numbers of inmates. When a literacy or language problem prevents an inmate from understanding the rule book, a staff member or interpreter can help the inmate understand the rules.

Clear, specific regulations should also help staff members understand and implement the inmate discipline policy consistently. Institutional personnel

who work with inmates usually receive periodic in-service training on the rules of inmate conduct, the rationale for the rules, and the sanctions available.

## Reporting Incidents

When very minor infractions or incidents occur, the officer has the option of informally resolving them. This should be done only in the case of very minor violations, to keep discipline consistent across the entire institution. Having too many informal resolutions can begin to erode overall control. Many institutions require a documenting memorandum for informal resolutions, so that supervisory staff can see patterns developing.

If a more serious incident occurs, most institutions require that an incident or disciplinary report of some kind be filed. The report describes the event itself in factual terms, and any unusual inmate behavior,

illegal, and they may be subject to established criminal penalties in addition to internal punishment. For that reason, when an inmate allegedly commits a criminal act, the case is often referred to the proper law enforcement officials, who decide whether or not to prosecute the individual.

There are also restrictions on how an inmate who may be charged criminally can be interviewed or interrogated, in order to preserve certain rights against self-incrimination in the criminal case. Agency policy spells out these restrictions, and they should be carefully observed.

## Segregating Inmates

Serious violations—such as arguments or fights, possession of escape paraphernalia, and many other incidents—may require removing inmates from their units or jobs to locked units. Administrative and disciplinary locked status (whether called segregation or detention) is necessary to maintain the institution's orderly operation. These housing statuses significantly restrict inmates in their movement and other personal freedoms, including possession of personal property and access to normal institutional programs. These units are used for the short- or long-term isolation of the most dangerous, troublesome, and escape-prone inmates—individuals believed to be a danger to staff or other inmates, or to the institution's security and orderly operation. These inmates need more supervision, and a higher frequency of searches and security inspections are required in these units. Staff here should be the first to be issued personal body alarms, in order to increase their personal safety.

Separate housing areas are ordinarily designated for these functions, units with vestibule or sallyport entrances, and special physical construction features. In an emergency, any housing unit can be designated as administrative or disciplinary status, and staffed and managed accordingly.

An officer usually may not simply take an inmate to a locked unit; a supervisor should be involved in the decision to remove an inmate from the population. Of course, in an emergency, individual staff members may do so in order to prevent a problem from growing, or to control a violent inmate. In this process, the officer must immediately search the inmates involved. In many institutions, the inmate is also placed in handcuffs to be moved to the locked unit.

In any case where an inmate is placed in locked status, a memorandum or incident report should be prepared, detailing the reason for the action. This report is usually given to the shift or watch supervisor, with copies to members of the inmate's unit or classification team, the supervisor of the locked unit, and to the inmate, so long as that is not a risk to institutional security.

witnesses (staff or inmate), physical evidence (weapons, property, etc.), or force used by either the inmate or officer during the incident. After signing the document, the officer forwards it to the designated correctional supervisor for investigation and further processing.

This report becomes the basis for further review of the episode, and possible disciplinary action. Not every report filed will result in further action; sometimes the supervisor or investigating officer will find a good reason to drop the charge, or to resolve it informally. In many other cases, however, the report is used as the basis for a due process hearing against the inmate, and a significant punishment may be imposed. This places an important responsibility on the reporting officer to be fair and accurate in preparing the report.

## When Prison Violations Are Crimes

Some internal institutional offenses also are state or federal crimes. Obviously, murder, assault, theft, and many other offenses committed by inmates are

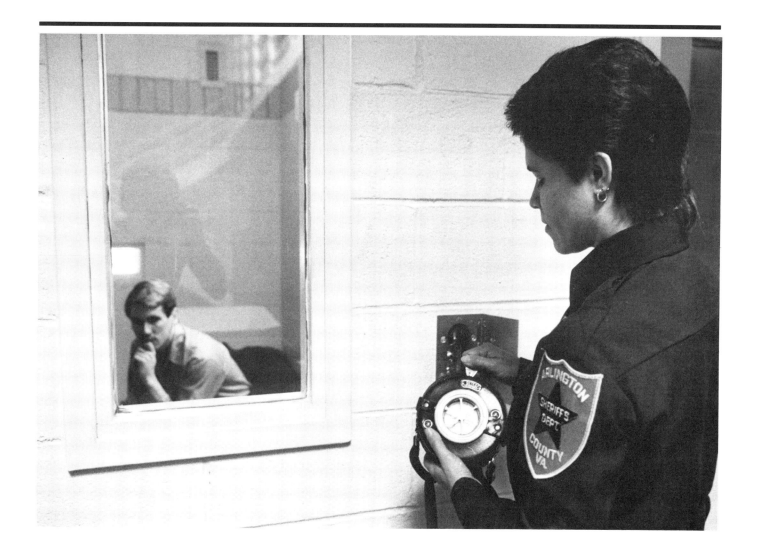

ACA standards establish clear requirements for the operation of a locked unit. Among them are providing basic hygiene items, as well as eyeglasses and writing materials. Inmates should also wear the same type of clothing as the general population, unless security clearly requires a distinct type of clothing, or unless it is for their protection, such as removing a belt to prevent a suicide attempt.

## Administrative Locked-Unit Status

Removing an inmate from the general prison population for a short time is an accepted correctional practice that requires no due process hearing. An inmate may be placed in administrative locked-unit status by the warden, disciplinary committee, shift supervisor, or members of an inmate's unit team, depending on the institution's specific policy. Ordinarily, an inmate in administrative locked status is permitted to retain most personal property items, but is locked in a cell for most of the day with limited access to recreation, television, showers, and other normal institutional activities.

*Reliable information, systematically collected and analyzed, helps in regularly supervising and managing the institution, and can prevent riots or other disturbances.*

Inmates may generally be placed in short-term administrative segregation for the following reasons:

- Awaiting or following a hearing on a violation of rules
- Awaiting an investigation or trial for committing a criminal act
- Awaiting transfer, or as a holdover between institutions
- For the inmates' protection

29

## Pending Classification

In some institutions, an inmate may be placed in administrative locked-unit status only if charged with an offense for which disciplinary locked status could be imposed, if he or she is found guilty of the offense. Local regulations spell out specific restrictions of this type.

In many institutions this same general category includes inmates requesting or requiring protection from others in the general population. They are subject to many of the same restrictions of other administrative-status inmates. However, court decisions have said that institutions must allow protective-custody cases to participate in as many of the usual programs as possible, as long as this imposes no threat to them or the institution's security. Care should be taken that inmates do not come to see placement in protective custody as desirable. Each case should be reviewed frequently, with the goal of ending the separate housing assignment as soon as possible.

## Disciplinary Locked-Unit Status

The use of disciplinary locked-unit housing is often the subject of considerable concern and litigation. Long-term segregation in disciplinary status generally is held by the courts to involve an inmate's liberty interests, and therefore requires due process protections in the form of some type of hearing. As a result, except for the most unusual circumstance, an inmate may be placed in disciplinary status only after a full due process hearing has been held, in which all rights have been provided. Disciplinary status is usually reserved for inmates found to have committed

major rule infractions for serious offenses, and then only for limited periods.

The due process hearing may be the result of a multilevel review process, involving investigators, unit staff review, a disciplinary committee, or a single designated disciplinary hearing officer. No matter what the actual procedure determined by agency policy, court decisions on due process outline the rights that must be provided in such a hearing, and they include:

- The right to be notified of charges before the hearing
- The right to call witnesses if they are reasonably available
- The right to present relevant evidence
- The right to receive assistance in preparing a response to the charges
- The right to appeal to an impartial third party

If found to have committed the prohibited act by the due process hearing, the inmate may be placed in disciplinary status. Other actions, such as losing good time, may also be taken.

In disciplinary status, the inmate has significantly fewer privileges than in administrative status. In most cases, everything except basic personal property is removed and stored, and access to all but basic programs and services may be reduced or stopped.

## General Locked-Unit Procedures

Locked units contain inmates who are potentially a danger to themselves, institutional security, staff, or other inmates. For that reason, procedures for either type of unit should include the same basic principles. While each institution has its own specific rules, the following procedures are common to most locked-unit operations.

All incoming inmates must be searched; their personal property must also be searched for contraband, and then inventoried, with a receipt given to the inmate. This inventory process safeguards staff against allegations of pilferage and theft, and also is a prime opportunity to remove items not permitted in the unit.

### Records

When any individual is moved to a locked unit, the following information must be recorded in the general unit log and other individual inmate records: name, number, originating housing unit, date admitted, type of infraction or reason for admission, tentative release date (if known), and any special medical or psychiatric problems or needs. All releases, incidents, and unusual inmate behavior should also be recorded in this general log and the individual inmate record kept in the unit.

The unit staff should maintain an individual record on each inmate, noting the following for each day: the time of meals, time and amount of recreation, showers, visits by medical staff, as well as any unusual inmate behavior or incidents, such as refusing recreation or meals. When the inmate is released from locked status, these individual records may then be sent to the inmate's central file, to serve as a permanent record of the period in locked status. They can be a valuable record in later court cases where inadequate care is alleged.

The unit should also maintain a visitor log, in which staff record the names, positions, and times of visits by all officials who inspect the units, counsel inmates, deliver medications, make medical rounds, or otherwise visit the unit for any reason.

Inmate workers or witnesses for disciplinary hearings coming into the unit from the general population must be kept to the necessary minimum, and searched both going in and coming out of the unit. These inmate workers must be supervised constantly, and their selection should be approved by a supervisor.

Tools kept in the unit, and those coming in with maintenance crews, must be inventoried and carefully controlled throughout the time they are in the unit. Only those tools required for a particular job should be permitted in the unit.

### Personal Property

Personal property is generally restricted to some degree in all locked units, and may be severely limited in disciplinary status. In either case, while an inmate is housed in a locked unit, supervisory staff may be authorized by policy to remove from an inmate's cell any item the inmate is likely to destroy or use to cause self-injury. However, in the case of personal care materials, the supervisor should permit the inmate to use the item while monitored by an officer, or find a suitably safe substitute.

Most institutions require that when an inmate is deprived of any item or activity usually authorized, that decision must be made with the approval of a supervisor; in many cases, a written report is required to detail the reason why the item was taken from the inmate. Ordinarily, copies of these reports are forwarded immediately to the chief correctional supervisor.

If circumstances appear to justify the removal of all personal items in a cell, approval should be obtained in advance from the warden or designee. No item or activity should be withheld longer than necessary to ensure the inmate's safety and the well-being of the staff and other inmates. In no case should an inmate be deprived of an item or activity for the sole purpose of punishment, without a due process hearing.

### Meals

Meals are ordinarily served in cells in these units. This guide's food service chapter gives additional information on this subject, but two important rules in all locked-unit operations are that inmates should not serve food to other inmates in these units, and food should not be used as a punishment. Allowing inmates to serve food is a prime opportunity for extortion, food tampering, or other problems. To avoid using food as a control measure, if an inmate throws food trays or food at staff, it may be necessary to prepare nutritionally adequate sack lunches that cannot be as readily used against staff. Inmates who plug their sinks and toilets may need to have the water in their cells controlled from the outside, but at no time should food or water be withheld as a punishment.

### Movement

Movement in restraints is a typical feature of most locked units. Any time an inmate in locked status is out of a cell and in contact with staff or other inmates,

# *Discipline is most effectively imposed when inmates believe the process is fair.*

he or she should be in handcuffs. This process requires handcuff ports in all cell doors, shower grilles, recreation cage doors, and any other areas where inmates may be cuffed or uncuffed. Local procedures describe how that is done, and whether it should be in front or behind.

## Group Activities

Careful control of recreation and other group activities is also a must in locked units. In many high-security settings, one-at-a-time recreation is the rule. In others, carefully selected small groups may recreate together. No matter what the arrangement, these groups should be under constant staff supervision, and the inmates should be restrained when they are in direct contact with staff.

## Searches

High-risk areas like locked units must be searched more often than other areas. These searches should be logged, so that a record of which cells and areas have been searched is available to staff on other shifts.

Recreation areas should be searched for contraband before and after each recreation period. In addition, all security hardware and the physical features of the area should be a part of the regular security inspection system, and in this case, should be inspected not less than daily.

Searches of inmate cells should be performed on a frequent but unpredictable basis. Some institutions regularly move inmates from cell to cell, in order to disrupt any attempt to tamper with or compromise the room's security.

Searches of common areas in the housing unit should be part of the regular security inspection program, with close supervisory review of all findings. Particular attention should be paid to the bars, locking devices, door guides, and metallic items that could be used to fabricate weapons, but no portion of the unit can be overlooked.

All cell and common area searches should be logged for reference by other staff and supervisory personnel.

## Visits

Visits for inmates in locked units are often conducted in the unit, or in a special controlled, noncontact visiting area in the regular visiting room. Because of the concern for high-security inmates in particular, special search and escort procedures may be in place for both inmates and visitors.

## Health and Hygiene

In general, all showers should be constructed with a grille door that can be locked, so that the inmate is safe in the shower from other inmates who may be moved out of their cells by staff, and also to safeguard staff from the inmate in the shower. In the case of inmates who present unusual management problems, the use of cells with built-in showers has been one solution.

Medical rounds are described in another chapter of this guide. It is important, however, that inmates in the locked units have access to equivalent medical services, and that staff not deny them necessary medical care.

## Services

Religious, educational, counseling, and other services are typically delivered to inmates in their unit. In many instances, this takes the form of staff members touring the unit regularly, and stopping at the cell fronts to discuss their problems. In the case of library and legal reference services, those materials are ordinarily requested from a central location. In some institutions, a small law library collection is maintained in the unit, and after requesting to be put on a schedule for using the area, the inmate can be locked in the room with the legal material.

## Summary

Supervision and fair, consistent discipline are the keys to maintaining not only internal institutional order, but public safety. No matter how secure the perimeter, if the interior of an institution is improperly supervised, eventually the inmates will find a way to breach the security.

*APPLICABLE ACA STANDARDS*

Records: 3-4092
Special Management Inmates: 3-4237 to 3-4261
Security and Control: 3-4180 and 3-4181
Inmate Rules and Discipline: 3-4214 to 3-4236, and 3-4243

# 5

# Security and Control

To maintain a secure institution, staff must prevent escapes, control contraband, and properly control inmate movement and activity. The necessary level of control is maintained through the hardware and physical security features of the institution, as well as through human action inside the perimeter. Of the two, the human factor is far more important; without it, the hardware would deteriorate and the physical plant, no matter how secure, could be defeated by the inmates.

That human factor is made up of well-trained and disciplined professional staff, using sound classification and discipline systems, and efficient communication methods. Coupled with those elements must be the willingness of managers to not only listen to problems of staff and inmates, but to effectively deal with them in a timely manner. This guide discusses the perimeter or external security issues first and then explains the importance of internal security measures and staff performance to overall institution security and control.

## External Controls

External controls are the institution's physical features that make up its perimeter and support structures. In secure facilities, towers, gates, fences, lights, detection systems, and walls are a major part of the physical security.

An institution's specific security features are determined by the kind of inmates it houses. ACA standards describe typical perimeter construction for maximum- or medium-security institutions as usually consisting of walls or fences, with buffer zones between buildings and the perimeter itself. Walls are typically capped by towers that overlook the interior of the compound. Fenced compounds ordinarily have freestanding towers of some sort, a mobile patrol system, or both. If double fences are used, they ordinarily are at least 12 feet high, and 20 to 30 feet apart, with rolled-wire reinforcements and the inner fence embedded in a concrete curb or barrier to prevent tunneling under it. The area between the fences should be sanitized to suppress weed growth and to allow officers better visibility.

A limited number of sallyports or gates, ideally no more than two, should penetrate the perimeter; gates are ordinarily operated from towers or other remote locations. These fence and gate configurations are used with various combinations of electronic surveillance devices—pressure, sound, closed-circuit television, and microwave-based systems.

It is highly desirable to have a buffer zone approximately 100 to 150 feet wide between both the inner fence and the institution's buildings, and the outer fence and adjacent buildings or tree lines. The inner zone prevents inmates from using any nearby buildings to their advantage in an escape; the larger the exterior buffer zone, the easier it is to respond safely with disabling gunfire should an inmate try to escape.

Minimum-security institutions ordinarily rely on single fences, or no fences at all. A mobile patrol may be used, but if inmates are screened appropriately, the patrol staff will be just as concerned about intruders bringing in contraband as inmates trying to escape.

In most older maximum- and medium-security institutions, towers form the backbone of perimeter security. They contain armed officers who observe a specific sector inside the perimeter. Tower officers are typically equipped with at least a rifle or shotgun, and may also have a sidearm and gas in the tower as well. Less commonly, institutions may have armed posts at critical points inside the compound, including a few prisons with armed staff in gun galleries or gun walks

Officers assigned to foot patrol adjacent to the perimeter must inspect all walls and buildings where inmates might dig holes, or hide tools, weapons, ropes, or homemade ladders. The fence or wall itself must be part of the regular security inspection system, as must all penetrating tunnels, manhole covers, and other security features.

### Pedestrian and Vehicular Traffic

Pedestrian and vehicular traffic may enter and leave only at designated points in the perimeter—the fewer the better. Where possible, these entrances are located close to one another; this reduces the number of ground-level officers required to check vehicles and visitors. All entrances and exits to the institution should be sallyported.

All visitors and employees must pass through a pedestrian entrance, gatehouse, or main entrance, where they are properly identified and processed into the secure portion of the institution. Larger institutions may have a separate sallyport near the vehicular gate designated for work crews. Officers at each gate must thoroughly search everyone who enters, and properly identify them as they come in and out of the institution.

Usually gates separate any public-access portions of the administration building from the secure part of the prison. Officers controlling these gates or grilles (usually in the control center) must admit and release only those employees, visitors, or inmates who are clearly authorized. Most institutions that have inmate workers in the administrative area use a gate pass system of some sort to positively identify all inmates permitted through this critical traffic point.

Vehicular sallyports are often controlled by an officer in an adjacent tower. Vehicles with materials, equipment, and supplies may not pass through until drivers are cleared by the appropriate official, or the authorizing paperwork has been produced and carefully validated. Every vehicle entering or leaving the vehicular entrance must be searched thoroughly—before admittance for contraband, and before leaving the secure compound for inmates who may be hiding in the payload or under the carriage.

The drivers of all vehicles should dismount and stand clear of the cab to demonstrate that they are not under any duress. In addition, the officer on the ground who performs the search should also stand well clear of the vehicle when giving the "all clear" signal to the tower, so that it is evident that they are

inside housing units. This is generally considered a more risky strategy than the policy adopted by most agencies, which is to never have firearms regularly stationed inside the institution.

In any case, these armed posts exist to deter and prevent escapes, or other incidents that could result in serious injury or even death to employees or inmates. Firearms should only be used when other means fail, and then only according to institutional policy. Staff should abide by specific agency policy in using deadly force. Ordinarily, the policy is to shout a warning before firing, then to fire a warning shot if needed. If the inmate still has not stopped the dangerous activity, then shots are to be fired to disable, rather than to kill.

### Post Orders

Each perimeter post should have a comprehensive set of post orders providing clear guidance to employees on the use of deadly force, hostage situations, actions regarding intruding civilians, and other situations. These post orders vary according to institutional size and security level, but they also typically indicate the location and use of surveillance devices, how mobile patrols fit into the perimeter security picture, firing distances for various points within the compound, inventory procedures for weapons and ammunition, and other important details.

Correctional officers may also be assigned to mounted or other motorized patrol duty outside the prison. These methods are used for supervising work details in remote areas, and discouraging contact between inmates working on outside details and civilians passing by.

not giving the signal under duress.

Occasionally the regular vehicular entrance is not suitable for serving large industrial operations, and a second sallyport is needed for incoming materials and outgoing products, or in some institutions to accommodate a train track for boxcars moved by a small switch engine. Depending on physical plant constraints, the entrance can also be used for emergency vehicles (hook and ladder truck, ambulance, etc.).

## Hostage Policy

However, it is extremely important that the staff assigned to gate operations be aware of the agency hostage policy. While this policy may vary in detail from one agency to another, in general, most correctional institutions hold to the rule that no hostage has any authority, and that no inmate will be released while holding another person—visitor, employee, or another inmate—under duress.

Tunnels penetrating the perimeter, usually for utility service, are a clear concern. They should be secured with multiple grilles; ideally, the grilles on the outside half of the tunnel should be keyed so that they can be opened only from the outside. These are

areas where technology can be used to good effect. The use of motion detection circuits on closed-circuit television cameras, acoustic monitoring devices, and other electronic systems can alert staff to unauthorized activity in critical tunnel areas. Drainpipes and other utility piping should be designed with a sufficiently small diameter, or should go through constrictions of some type, to prevent their use in an escape attempt.

*In addition to the perimeter security that is obvious to the casual observer, every activity in an institution has an impact on security, and can be important in preventing escapes and disorder.*

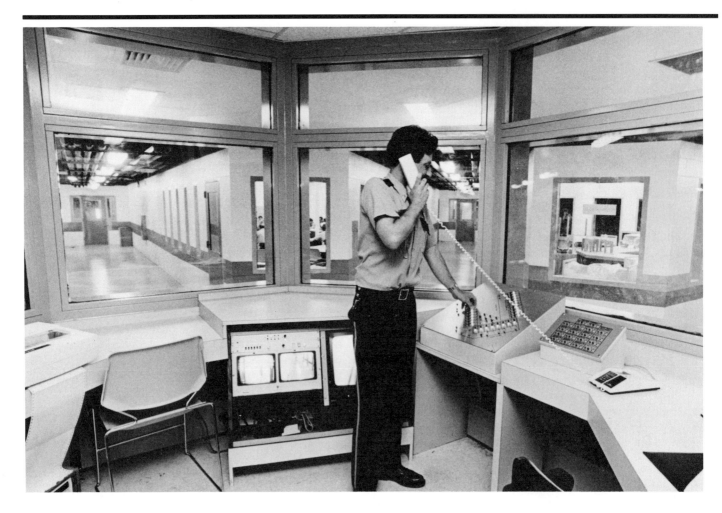

## Lighting

Lighting on the perimeter and compound is vitally important. The proper amount of lighting can greatly aid tower and patrol staff. Correct placement of lights in the interior eliminates blind spots in the shadow of buildings, makes internal patrols safer for staff, and reduces inmates' ability to move about in a nighttime escape attempt. Institutions are increasingly using high-intensity, high-mast lighting that provides lighting levels and coverage far superior to regular mercury or quartz vapor fixtures on standard light poles.

## Outside-Assisted Escape Attempts

Escape attempts with outside assistance typically take a relatively predictable form; a visitor brings in a weapon, disguise, or some other contraband to assist the inmate, or may be waiting outside the perimeter with a vehicle. However, staff must be constantly alert for other variations on these methods.

There have been, for instance, incidents where outside parties have fired on institutional towers with high-powered weapons while inmates inside attempted to escape. There is always the possibility of an outsider throwing a weapon over a fence, and the inmate involved using the weapon against staff. These escape strategies, too, must be anticipated in yard search and outside patrol procedures.

Helicopter-assisted escapes are a relatively new innovation for prisons, but a serious one nonetheless. Correctional agencies do not agree on the proper policy in this area. Several schools of thought have emerged. The first involves the use of ground "clutter," such as using trees and light poles on the compound, to make it more difficult for a helicopter to successfully land. This method has been extended by stringing wires from buildings and poles throughout the compound, to further complicate low-level hovering.

The use of firearms against helicopters is a particularly difficult issue. Some agencies permit firing on an inmate trying to run to a helicopter, but not the helicopter itself, because if it subsequently crashed, the possibility of an explosion could endanger perhaps hundreds of nonparticipating inmates, and even staff. If a rotor blade was hit, it could also spray the yard area with shrapnel-like fragments that could kill nonparticipants. At least one location has its towers equipped with Bridger line guns, which are used in naval operations to project lines from one ship to another. In a prison application, they could be fired from a tower, over a helicopter's rotor, to tangle it and render the craft unmaneuverable. Other locations have simply taken the position that staff should do no more than note the identifying features of the aircraft, and depend on law enforcement and military aircraft

to trail the escapees. In any case, officers should be familiar with the policy of their particular agency on this important subject.

## Internal Controls

After an institution's physical perimeter is secure, attention must turn to the interior. Escapes will inevitably take place, even with a secure perimeter, if inmates are not prevented from making or acquiring contraband, compromising internal security hardware, or moving at will without staff accounting for them. In truth, an institution is only as secure as its employees make it on the inside.

Inmate discipline is discussed elsewhere in this guide, but it is important to note the role that it plays in security and control. Staff must have an effective disciplinary system at their disposal for dealing with troublemakers and escape-prone inmates. If the inmate discipline system breaks down, it is almost inevitable that security will break down also.

Supervisory visibility is one of the central reasons why well-managed institutions run that way. The standards and expectations that top staff convey in the security and control area are absolutely vital. If

they are active in touring the institution, talking to staff and inmates and thereby staying familiar with the institution and its climate, then security and control are far more likely to be intact.

Staff need clear, written guidelines to direct them. Each institution or correctional system should have a security manual that outlines security procedures. Topics should include security inspections, inmate counts, control of weapons and chemical agents, suppression of contraband, key and tool control, as well as cell equipment, emergency procedures, and supervision of inmate programs and activities. This manual of policies and procedures should be available to all staff, and be used as the basis for annual refresher training. In addition, the manual should be the starting point for any internal agency review of procedural or policy compliance, through a structured audit program.

## Design Issues

There are some internal physical plant items that greatly contribute to security and control. The importance of the control center cannot be overemphasized. Ideally, the control center is outside the secure perimeter, away from direct inmate activity. It is the center of all communication functions and is staffed around the clock. Staff here monitor key traffic points, take inmate counts, issue and inventory keys,

and coordinate internal and perimeter security networks. They monitor various systems—fire alarm, public address, smoke and thermal detection, radios, Teletype, computers, walk and perimeter lighting, and other mechanical and electrical systems. All of these mechanical systems must be tested on a regular basis, and the results of those tests logged. Gas and other equipment should be maintained on an inventory, checked regularly, and outdated items replaced with fresh supplies.

The control center must be the institution's most secure location—completely invulnerable to inmate attack. In addition to ballistics-grade glazing in all windows, it should have bars over the windows, to further resist attack by rioting inmates. All walls and ceilings should be of reinforced construction, and the control center should have independent power and ventilation systems that enable it to continue operations in the event of a widespread institution takeover. The entrance should have an interlocked, double-door sallyport that ensures that only authorized personnel enter. Often, counts are taken in the control center, and keys are issued from this point.

### Housing Units

The construction of housing units has a great deal to do with the degree of supervision that can be exerted in an institution. Facilities with dormitories generally are far more difficult to control than those with single cells, at least from the standpoint of the officer in the housing area. On the other hand, even a dormitory may be better than a single-cell housing unit that is so poorly designed that there are blind corners and hiding places where inmates can be totally out of an officer's sight. In short, there can be difficulties in either kind of housing area. Staff need to learn the weaknesses of their particular design, and find ways to compensate, either through procedures, additional staff, or additional technology.

### Internal Movement

Physical design can also affect internal movement control by preventing inmate access to unauthorized areas. Control can be facilitated by such means as cutoff fences on the yard and at the ends of blind courtyards between buildings. It also can be maintained through manned checkpoints with fixed metal detection equipment, where staff stop inmates, search them, and check passes. It also can be obtained through closed-circuit camera coverage of key locations where staff cannot be posted. Each of these strategies and many others prevent inmates from moving to areas where they can pursue unauthorized activities.

### Entrances

The entrances to buildings and program and recreation areas are other posts that can be used effectively to monitor and control inmate traffic. In addition, the construction and location of windows, doors, mirrors, closed-circuit television, stairwells, elevators, and other physical features of buildings can greatly affect internal building supervision. The use of cutoff grilles in corridors and crash doors in units can be an effective traffic control device, particularly in an emergency, when staff need to gain additional time to contain a situation.

## Inmate Accountability

Inmate accountability is far more than simply counting inmates. It involves movement control, pass systems, census checks, and record systems also.

Every correctional institution must have a system for positively accounting for its inmates. A well-designed system includes strict accountability for inmates assigned to all areas inside the facility, on outside details, as well as on furlough or other approved, temporary absences.

There should be at least one official count each shift, and most institutions count inmates formally at least five times daily. The most common times are before and after typical working hours and at bedtime, coupled with two or more counts during the night, when the inmates are locked in their cells or dormitories. During those counts, inmates must be in place, and not move from one point to another. As much as possible, all inmates should be in their assigned housing unit, in their cells or at their bunks, during the count.

When officers count a unit, they must be sure that they actually see each inmate. Inmates who sleep under the covers may have to be disturbed just enough to be sure they are in fact there, and that a dummy is not in the bed. In dormitory units, two officers must be present, one to count and one to back up and be sure no inmate "bed-hopping" occurs to cover for a missing inmate.

### Outcounts

Inmates whose jobs require them to be out of the housing unit during counts are on what is usually called "outcount" to that job area. The staff member in the work area must submit the names and numbers of those inmates in writing to a supervisor for approval, usually at least one hour before the time of the count. Those inmates are then approved, and the officer taking the count is given the signed, approved outcount approval form for the count records.

Counts made as outcounts on the job site are done differently than in a housing unit, where inmates are required to be in their immediate living areas or cells. On-the-job counts require that all inmates assemble in one area to be counted by staff. The numbers are called in, just like those from a unit, and recount procedures are also the same. Inmates may move about in the work area after the count has cleared by telephone, but they may not leave the area until the entire institutional count is cleared.

The count numbers for each unit are called in to the control center. If the count is correct, inmates in the unit may move about, but they may not be released from the unit until the entire institutional count has cleared. The officers counting must submit a signed count slip, attesting to the count they called in by telephone. In the event an officer calls in an incorrect number, a recount of that unit must be conducted, and local policy may require multiple recounts to verify the actual number.

The count is ordinarily taken in the control center or designated count room. The officer maintaining the master count record is provided up-to-the-minute information throughout the day on all inmate housing moves, work assignment changes, admissions to the

hospital, etc. All inmates in legal custody are included in the master count and there is a written record of all temporary absences from the facility. In effect, the count officer must continually know where every inmate is, and how many inmates are in each unit. This ongoing count process is necessary for another reason; if an escape occurs, the count records in the control center must be used as the basis for an emergency count. In addition, count records should be retained in enough detail to reconstruct any count held in the last 30 days, should there be any question about a particular count.

On the job or in the cellhouse, accountability is somewhat different, because official counts are not ordinarily held during working hours. Instead, crews are checked at the beginning and end of work periods against the assigned detail roster or using some other system such as a crew kit card. Job supervisors as well as unit officers also take informal counts, or census checks, which are frequent but irregular checks made to verify all inmates are present. Unless otherwise required, reports of these counts are made only when an inmate is missing.

---

*Most correctional institutions hold to the rule that no hostage has any authority, and that no inmate will be released while holding another person under duress.*

### Inmate Movement

Correctional officers are often required to transport inmates between institutions or to and from other locations outside the institution. The officer in charge ordinarily verifies the identity of all inmates as they board the vehicle, and verifies the count onboard each time the vehicle stops and starts. Policies and procedures are designed to guard against escape. Restraints are ordinarily used for all but minimum-security cases.

Line counts may be used to count work details and other large groups out of housing units. To avoid being distracted by inmates, officers should conduct line counts from behind. Large details usually are easier to count when inmates are assembled in columns of two.

Restrictions on inmate movement may vary depending on the classification of inmates and the

type of institution. Written procedures ordinarily specify how officers regulate inmates moving from area to area, using a combination of pass systems, telephone contacts, intercoms, or other methods.

To these should be added the use of well-designed record systems, such as unit identification and assignment cards, inmate crew kits for work details, control center cards and pictures, and gate passes. These internal identification structures help staff control inmate activities and movement in the institution. A related category is the need to maintain central file pictures that are kept current for use in escape flyers, in the event an inmate successfully escapes from the facility.

## Searches and Contraband Control

To detect and prevent the accumulation of contraband, institutions must conduct frequent unannounced searches of inmates, their property and quarters, and other areas of the facility. A comprehensive search program can detect and prevent the introduction of contraband, recover missing or stolen property, and help prevent escapes and other disturbances.

Although contraband is defined differently in each correctional system, in general, it is any item not authorized to be received by an inmate, sold in the institution, or received from the outside, as well as any otherwise approved item that has been modified in an unapproved manner. Contraband can be sold or traded (as in the case of drugs), or it can be used for aiding in an escape attempt, destroying property, or endangering human life. Carrying or possessing contraband is a violation of institutional rules. The local definition of contraband should be included in the admission and orientation program and in any inmate handbook used in that program.

ACA standards stress the need for a written policy regarding searches of facilities and inmates in order to control illegal articles. Frequent searches of inmates and their living areas are not conducted to harass or agitate inmates. They are a basic responsibility of institution staff, and are necessary to discover and eliminate contraband. However, abusing the power to reasonably search inmates may result in courts restricting the use of specific search procedures. As a result, staff should be well trained in policies regarding searches, and those documents should be reviewed at least annually and updated if necessary.

Generally, search procedures will not be questioned if the officers conducting them are professional and considerate of inmates and their possessions. However, problems can occur when officers use abusive, ill-timed methods; those tactics can cause inmate grievances, disturbances, or litigation. Repeated confiscation of articles properly belonging to inmates, even though later returned, is certain to cause resentment. At the same time, an officer should not neglect examining an article simply because it is not considered contraband. Some innocent-appearing objects can be converted into dangerous weapons or hiding places for drugs.

Preventive measures to keep contraband out of an institution begin at the institution's perimeter—the walls or fences. These must be adequately guarded and patrolled. However, most search activity is conducted inside the institution.

## Individual Inmate Searches

The technique used in searching inmates is important; officers must avoid using unnecessary force, or otherwise embarrassing or humiliating them. Good search techniques are best learned by doing searches; however, during routine "patdowns," officers generally do the following:

- Require inmates to remove hats, unbutton coats

or jackets, and empty all personal articles from pockets
- Working from behind, run hands under the inmate's shirt collar and down the upper part of each arm to the wrists
- Bring hands back along the undersides of arms to the armpits
- Sweep hands down from the shirt front to the belt
- Run thumbs around the inside of the belt from front to back
- Run hands down front of legs to shoe tops and up the back side of legs
- Sweep hands down the back from the shirt collar to the waist
- Examine subject's hat and other personal articles, including the inside of the hatband, cigarette cases, glasses cases, or anything that appears unusual

### Body Searches

Unless it is an emergency, body or "strip" searches should take place in a private area, such as in a booth or behind a curtain. Officers should stand behind the person being searched, unless the inmate is in restraints.

The technique generally involves the following: The staff member directs the inmate to remove all clothing, dentures, and prostheses (false limbs), and to move away from the clothing, which should be searched for any concealed contraband. The officer should then visually inspect the inmate's entire body, looking for contraband; the inmate should be required to open his or her mouth and allow the officer to look inside for concealed items.

This procedure should include directing the inmate to lift his or her arms to expose the armpits, lift each foot to expose the soles of the feet and to allow inspection between the toes, and bend over and spread the buttocks to ensure nothing obvious has been concealed in the crotch or in the rectum.

An inspection of an inmate's body cavities only takes place if there is reasonable belief that the inmate is carrying contraband. Inspection of body cavities, such as the nasal cavities, rectum, or vagina, whether manually or by instrument, should only be conducted with good cause, and when authorized by the warden or designee. It must be conducted in private, by health care personnel or other staff who have been specifically trained in these procedures.

When officers search a large group of inmates, such as a work detail, they should order the inmates to line up and present themselves one at a time for search. The first person searched then forms the start of a new line far enough from the unsearched people to prevent the passing of contraband. After the searches are complete, the officer should scan the area where the inmates stood to locate any contraband that may have been dropped or discarded.

## Housing Unit Searches

Searches of housing units, cells, or rooms should be performed without warning and irregularly. Cells should always be searched before being occupied by new inmates.

Ideally, two officers conduct room searches, taking care to leave a room in the same condition it was found in. Inmate property must be respected and not willfully discarded, broken, or misplaced. Officers doubting whether or not an item is contraband should consult the institutional rule book or a supervising officer.

Although it is impossible to list every hiding place for contraband, the following are the most obvious places in which officers look:

- Holes or cracks in the wall, floors, and ceilings
- Lighting and wall fixtures; any items mounted on the wall, such as outlets, conduits, etc.
- Washbowl, toilet, and plumbing stacks
- Shelves, drawers, and medicine cabinets as well as the contents
- Bedclothes, pillows, mattresses, and blankets
- Books, magazines, and newspapers
- False bottoms on large tobacco cans, ashtrays, drawers, or medicine cabinets
- Hollow legs of beds and other metal furniture
- Window bars, window frames, and overhead ventilators
- Sliding doors and grooves

Some critical areas, like locked units and their recreation areas, must be searched more often than other sections of the institution.

In conducting searches in rooms, but in any other area as well, staff should be alert for bombs and booby traps. A suspected bomb should not be touched. Supervisory staff should be called at once, and the institutional bomb plan put into effect. Another hazard of searching is the possibility of being stuck by hidden needles used by inmates for drug injection. Since these needles can carry the AIDS virus, great caution should be taken if any needles or syringes are discovered during a search.

## Contraband Disposal

In most cases, officers are required to submit a disciplinary report on any inmates possessing contraband on their person or in their personal living area. All items confiscated during searches should be properly secured, in line with local procedures that normally require a report documenting the circumstances under which the contraband was found. This report is ordinarily submitted to the appropriate supervisor, who disposes of it and the contraband.

In most institutions, there is some type of secure contraband locker, where items are held for evidence pending a disciplinary hearing, or for possible criminal action. These items are disposed of outside the institution at regular intervals when they are no longer needed. Local procedures describe how items with evidentiary value for a criminal case must be handled in order to preserve the "chain of custody" that proves that a certain item at trial is actually the item taken from the inmate.

## Vehicle Searches

All vehicles and machinery must be searched thoroughly when entering or leaving the institution. Because people and contraband can be concealed in a very small space, an effective vehicle search process includes careful inspection of passenger and freight compartments, motor compartments, and the undersides or suspension gear. Mirrors, "creepers," and even inspection pits can help ensure the undercarriage is inspected thoroughly. Inspections also may include removing hubcaps, examining spare tires, and inspecting dashes, seats, and head and door linings.

Commercial vehicles must be searched, and the driver's records listing the contents checked against the actual payload. If the list of cargo includes any narcotics, pharmaceutical supplies, gas equipment, arms, ammunition, or equally dangerous substances, the vehicle is ordinarily not allowed inside the institution. Any such items intended for the institution are unloaded outside, and then taken by staff to the designated storage area.

All shipments leaving the institution must be well searched also. Barrels or tanks of liquids and loads of loose materials, such as hay, grain, and refuse, are usually probed with a rod to detect any hidden inmates. Large boxes and crates are accompanied through the gate by the officer who supervised their packing, or are locked in storage until after the institutional count and before being loaded onto trucks or freight cars. Another option is to lock the entire vehicle in the sallyport through one or more counts.

## Searches in Connection with Visiting

Visitors must be searched before being allowed to enter the institution. This search ordinarily is limited to passing through a metal detection device, and depositing all packages, bags, purses, and other property in a locker or other designated storage area. A sign indicating the institution's policy on contraband and other restrictions should be displayed prominently and read by all visitors, who may be required to sign an acknowledgment form regarding the notice before entering.

Visitors are not ordinarily required to submit to a body search unless they volunteer for it. If staff strongly suspect that visitors possess contraband, the officer processing them should consult with a supervisor, who may deny the visit or even call for local law enforcement officers to investigate. Each agency has different regulations on detaining visitors in such cases, and staff processing visitors should be familiar with those rules, in order to avoid unlawfully detaining a visitor. Inmates should be searched before and after visits, to prevent them from bringing contraband into the visiting room, or taking anything obtained from a visitor back to the compound. In most institutions there is a sallyport-type vestibule area between the visiting room and the general-population area where inmates are given a visual body search before and after each visit. Most institutions also limit the amount of property permitted into the visiting room, and some require the inmates to wear a special jumpsuit and shoes, to reduce the likelihood of concealing contraband in standard institutional clothing during a visit.

Immediately before and after visiting hours, officers must conduct a thorough search of the visiting room for contraband, and inmates must not be permitted in the area during this search. During the visit, officers should watch for outside visitors passing illegal items to inmates, cross-visiting between inmates, and any attempt to exchange clothing or

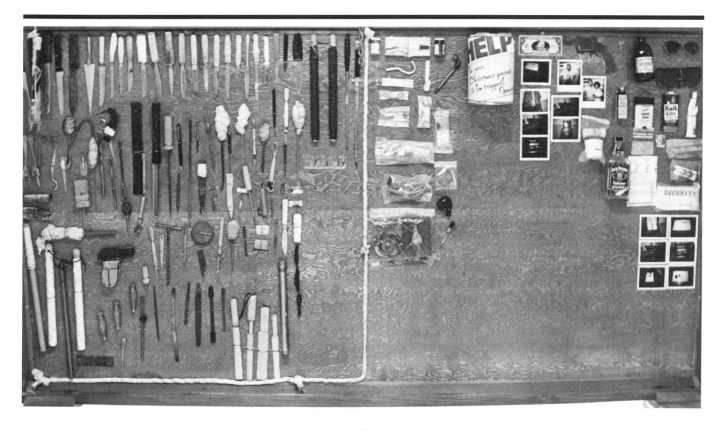

engage in sexual activity. Local regulations describe the kind of items that may legally pass between an inmate and a visitor, such as legal materials during an attorney's visit. After the visit, all trash left in the visiting area should be removed by staff and disposed of outside the institution, in order to prevent inmate workers from retrieving concealed contraband. Rest rooms should be searched thoroughly before and after visiting hours. Sinks, towel dispensers, and toilets should be given careful attention, because they could be used to hide contraband that could later be picked up by inmate janitors.

## Tool Control

Every item in a prison must be considered a potential weapon, including work tools, kitchen utensils, and maintenance supplies. This is particularly true of tools, and as a result, staff must supervise and control all tools very carefully. The procedures for handling, storing, and monitoring all equipment, as well as securing certain "hot items," are usually outlined in the local tool control policy, and are specific to each institution. However, as in many other areas, most institutions use some common procedures.

First, there must be a central authority, usually in the form of a tool control officer, who coordinates the purchase and control of all tools. Employees in most institutions are not permitted to purchase tools independently, or to bring their own tools into the institution.

# *Tools must be accounted for at all times.*

Tools must be accounted for at all times. This is done by maintaining a written inventory on each set of tools, and prominently posting the inventory where the tools are stored. This inventory must be checked daily by the responsible employee and verified at least monthly with a member of the correctional force.

Tools are generally classified into two or three categories:

*Class A Tools (Extremely Hazardous).* This includes hacksaws and blades, cutting torches, torch-cutting tips, large pipe wrenches, knives, bolt cutters, axes, and hypodermic needles and syringes. Portable welding equipment is ordinarily removed from the institution each day; if removing it is impossible, the

equipment should be kept in the institution's most secure area, with the tips and mixing chambers removed. Class A tools are issued only to employees; these items must be used under direct staff supervision at all times.

*Class B Tools (Hazardous).* These tools include items such as shovels, picks, and hammers that could be used to effect an escape but are less hazardous than Class A tools. Class B tools may be used by inmates under intermittent supervision.

*Class C Tools (Nonhazardous).* These tools are not considered hazardous and include small hand tools that cannot be used as weapons and are not considered contraband. (Some institutions combine Classes B and C into a single Class B category.)

### *Tool Storage*

Tools should be stored on shadow boards, with each space on the board either covered with a tool or a receipt for a tool; only one tool should be stored per shadow. Shadow boards containing any Class A tools must be locked in a secure room or tool crib. Items not adaptable to shadow boards should be kept in locked drawers or cabinets in a secure area.

Bolt cutters should be stored in the control center or armory and issued only when needed. Because of AIDS, hypodermic needles and syringes must be carefully handled, and used needle disposal must be handled according to procedures established jointly with the appropriate health officials.

All tools should be marked with numbers or symbols etched on them, so that a missing tool can be easily identified. Any missing tools should be reported immediately to the proper superior officer and an effort made to locate the equipment before inmates leave the area.

Broken or otherwise unserviceable tools should not be discarded directly; they should be exchanged for a replacement item, and the old tool disposed of outside the institution.

## Food Service Items

When not in use, Class A items, such as butcher knives, vegetable knives, meat and bone saws, skewers, cleavers, and ice picks, must be locked in a shadow-board storage cabinet, which should be in a locked room. These items are issued by the kitchen steward or officer, who records the name of the inmate to whom the knife or other tool is issued. Before the kitchen closes or a shift changes, the items should be checked.

Foods such as yeast, nutmeg, sugar, and mace are kept under lock and key, and used only under employee supervision. Extracts with an alcoholic base should not be used, but if their use is unavoidable, they too must be secured.

## Hospital Items

Surgical instruments (such as scalpels) are considered Class A tools, and doctors and dentists must be aware of the dangers of these items falling into inmate hands. A regular inventory procedure should be in place for these items, as for any other Class A tool.

Bulk supplies of medications such as psychotropics (usually medication for mental health cases), morphine, codeine, barbiturates, and tranquilizers, if kept in the institution, must be locked in a safe or vault, with the combination given to only certain officials. If daily use quantities must be kept available for emergencies, they should be in a relatively secure container, with shift-to-shift accountability maintained. When these items are used, they can be replenished from the separate bulk supply area or vault, which must be jointly inventoried by medical and correctional staff members at least once a month.

Any hazardous or toxic fluids, or those that may be sniffed, must also be inventoried and secured. These include flammables, carbon tetrachloride, degreasing compounds, some duplicating fluids, and all aerosol cans.

## Lock and Key Control

Along with inmate accountability and tool control, absolute control of all keys is a must for any institution. Very elaborate systems are necessary to ensure that keys do not fall into inmate hands.

Keys are usually issued from a central control area, where they are returned daily and accounted for constantly. Keys are stored so that their presence or absence is easily determined, usually on some form of key board, which uses a durable receipt or "chit" system to account for who has each set of keys at any moment. Key hooks in the control center should not have more than one ring on them; otherwise it is impossible to have accurate, prompt key accountability.

### Key Records

Key records are maintained to cross-index all keys alphabetically, numerically, and against key ring numbers. Cross-indexing of this type provides a structured method of controlling and inventorying all

key blanks and pattern keys in the institution. Records must be maintained that will show which keys are on each ring, which lock each key fits, and where each lock in the institution is in use. Keys opening multiple locks must be identifiable so that if one is lost, it will be immediately evident which locks must be changed.

Key rings, once assembled, should be marked with a tag that identifies the ring itself by a distinctive alphabetical and numerical code, as well as a tag that indicates the number of keys on the ring.

All keys in use in the institution—both those in regular circulation and emergency keys—should have the split rings soldered or spot-welded closed, to prevent tampering or removal. This measure helps ensure accurate key counts, and also eliminates the temptation for staff to remove a key from a ring to loan to another individual for a short time.

Once during each working day, preferably during the morning watch, all key rings should be reconciled as to count, in order to ensure that no keys have been lost or stolen. Employees who have keys on their person at that time should call their key count into the control center, and the control center officer should count all the keys on the key board to obtain a key total.

### Emergency Keys

The emergency key system enables staff to access every part of the institution rapidly to respond to a riot, fire, or any other crisis. The system must be clearly separate from all other keys on the central key board. Each set of emergency keys should take staff from the perimeter, or whatever starting point is

as well as the armory and control center themselves. These keys should be issued only on the authorization of the watch commander or some other senior staff member, and the issuance of the keys should be logged by the control center officer.

No restricted or emergency keys should leave the institution, and local procedures and staff supervision should enforce that requirement.

### Key Handling

The following general rules apply to key handling:

• Keys should never be thrown, or left in a lock; staff should carry key rings on a secure belt keeper or chain, to prevent loss.
• Entrance keys should never come inside the facility; to do so constitutes a serious security violation.
• Keys to the armory should never come in direct contact with inmates.
• Grand master keys should never be in open circulation inside the institution. The loss of just one of these keys could require a total overhaul of the key system, or at a minimum, rekeying major portions of the facility.
• Employees should only in rare instances be issued keys for their personal key rings, and even then a security key should not be taken home. The number of keys maintained on personal key rings should be reduced to an absolute minimum.
• Inmates ordinarily are not permitted to have keys other than those for personal lockers, living quarters, or work assignments, when appropriate. They should never carry security keys or be permitted to closely see the security key profiles.

## Security Inspections

It does not take long for inmates to become aware of security breaches and to find ways to take advantage of them. A functional security inspection procedure in an institution will prevent this from happening.

A typical security inspection system includes thorough searches of all physical security features of pre-identified zones by a specific staff member.

designated for that set, through every necessary door in that part of the institution. Various systems are in use, using color codes, metal tags, etching on the shank of the key, and other variations, which enable staff to quickly determine which key opens a given lock. Whatever system is adopted, all staff must be trained in it, so that in a crisis, anyone issued any set of keys can use them quickly and easily.

Regular issue keys should be rotated into and out of the emergency key rings to ensure that wear on the locks and keys is even. In addition, all emergency keys need to be tested periodically, not only by the locksmith but by other staff, to ensure that personnel unfamiliar with the peculiarities of the locks involved can operate them effectively. Also, supervisory personnel need to be trained to use the emergency keys. Ideally, a backup set of emergency key rings should be located either in the armory or one of the towers, for safekeeping.

### Restricted Keys

In addition to the emergency key system, a number of areas should be accessed only by restricted keys. These include the laundry and clothing issue, business office, personnel office, commissary, warehouses, and many of the administrators' offices,

General, nondefinitive inspections cannot substitute for specific checks, for which specific staff are responsible and accountable. Checks must be made for compromised bars, windows, locks, manhole covers, and other modified, inoperative, or tampered security features. Bars should be tapped regularly, locks tested, and other security devices checked. Security inspections must be paralleled by a scheduled maintenance procedure that ensures that all locks, windows, doors, and other security devices are fully operational.

Each inspection must be followed by a signed, documented report of the inspection, which is maintained on record for not less than 30 days. Supervisory personnel should have a list of the employees responsible for each inspection zone, and follow up immediately if an inspection form is not turned in.

## Communications

From a technological point of view, effective communication systems make it possible for officers to be in constant touch with each other. These systems include radios, tower intercoms, personal body alarms, and closed-circuit television. The way that each institution uses these technologies may differ in detail, but their general use is fairly consistent in most institutions.

Good communications in the nontechnical sense also help managers to make critical day-to-day operational decisions. As discussed in Chapter 4, they also ensure staff and inmates know policies and procedures, and that staff learn about changing policies before the inmates do. Clear information, circulated widely to staff and inmates, reduces the chance of day-to-day problems and larger disturbances. Good post orders and other internal information systems are the key to a well-informed, effective staff.

## Handling High-Security Inmates

Special precautions may be in order when unusually high-security cases are known to be in an institution. In many instances, this kind of inmate will be held in a special housing unit. Procedures there may include issuing an order for two or three staff, so that extra staff are available when the inmate is out of the cell.

In other instances, the inmate may be in the general population, and other precautions are necessary. A special information file, with pictures, may be set up in an area inaccessible to inmates. This file allows employees to review the backgrounds of these individuals, as well as others who present special management concerns. Housing assignments should be restricted to the most secure units. Work assignments should be selected with great care; if possible, tower officers supervising the immediate work area should know the identity of all high-security risk cases in that area. In general, inmates in this category should receive extra supervision by all staff.

## Special Supervision Units

Certain units in some institutions operate totally on a high-security basis. Locked housing units for administrative and disciplinary cases are one example. But there are several other categories that should be mentioned.

*Inmate accountability is far more than simply counting inmates. It involves movement control, pass systems, census checks, and record systems also.*

Special management units or control units are used to confine inmates who have demonstrated they are so dangerous, predatory, or violent that they cannot be successfully or safely held in the general population of any regular institution. These inmates are held in some systems in a separate locked unit that resembles administrative locked status, except that they are confined there for very long periods. In most cases, a due process hearing is required to place an inmate in this kind of unit, and special classification and review procedures are in place to determine when an inmate is ready for release.

Protective custody units have been mentioned, but it should be noted that many of these units are operated in a locked-unit setting. Even so, inmates in this category are to be provided approximately the same privileges and access to programs as nonprotective custody cases, to the degree that institutional security and their personal safety needs permit.

Witness security units are a special type of protective custody unit. While inmates in regular protective custody status may have provided information in a variety of ways, true witness security programs are for inmates who have actually provided testimony in exchange for a formal agreement that the government will protect them during confinement. The level of program and services in these units is ordinarily above those found in typical locked or protective custody units.

Inmates sentenced to death may be held in a separate section of a regular administrative locked unit, or they can be in a separate locked unit. Some systems even permit selected inmates under a death sentence to be in a non-locked unit. In a locked-unit environment, however, these inmates should be handled as extremely high-risk cases, and staff should be constantly aware of the possibility of a serious incident when dealing with an inmate who presumably has nothing to lose in an escape attempt or hostage takeover of a unit.

## Summary

Security and control are prime responsibilities of institutions and their staff. In addition to the perimeter security that is obvious to the casual observer, every activity in an institution has an impact on security, and can be important in preventing escapes and disorder. If adequate procedures are not in place and carefully followed inside the institution, then public safety and that of staff and inmates can be threatened.

Additional information on these subjects can be found in other ACA publications, particularly *Guidelines for Development of a Security Program* and the *Design Guide for Secure Adult Facilities*.

*APPLICABLE ACA STANDARDS*

Administration, Organization and Management: 3-4004 and 3-4011 to 3-4017
Safety and Emergency Procedures: 3-4164
Security and Control: 3-4167 to 3-4198

# 6

# Firearms, Gas, and Use of Force

Using deadly force or armed intervention in a crisis is a serious step requiring clearly established policy, well-trained staff, and sound judgment. Even the use of unarmed force can present serious problems if not done properly. All correctional officers should be well-versed in the policies and procedures for their particular agency in these areas, so that if and when the use of force becomes necessary, it will be done in an effective but properly restrained manner.

## Procedures and Authority for Use

Weapons and other security equipment (such as shields, batons, helmets, gloves, and body protectors) used in a correctional institution are chosen by administrators based on the physical plant and the number and type of inmates in the facility. Because of the inherent risk in their use, carefully developed policies and procedures specify who may be issued weapons, as well as how this equipment should be used. Agency and institution policy should clearly spell out all armory, weapon, and use-of-force practices.

The institution's armory should be in a totally secure location, ideally outside the facility's perimeter. It should have a double-door entry, and a pass-through or "dutch door" arrangement for issuing equipment in an emergency. The armory should be climate-controlled, have sufficient storage space for all weapons and ammunition, and have a telephone and a battery-powered emergency lighting system.

The authority for using weapons and force is ordinarily found in state or federal law and in specific agency policy. Detailed procedures for storing, handling, and accounting for weapons in continuous use in towers and patrol posts should be spelled out

in the post orders for these posts, as it should for inspecting weapons and counting ammunition when first assuming a post. With the tremendous variation in types of armed posts, it is impractical to describe these procedures in any detail. However, this chapter describes a number of the more common issues and practices encountered in typical prison settings.

## Weapon Storage and Upkeep

In most correctional systems, weapons and gas equipment are stored in secure areas that are not inaccessible to inmates but easily accessible to personnel in emergencies. Small amounts of tear gas, a few batons, and shields may be stored in the control center for emergencies, but for the most part, these items should be kept in the armory or a secure location outside the perimeter, such as a tower.

In a few institutions, weapons are maintained on armed posts inside the perimeter; storage and handling procedures at those locations are quite different. Because of the relatively few locations that do this, these procedures will not be described in this guide; local policies should be carefully followed at those institutions.

Storage of all ammunition and gas munitions should be in suitable metal cabinets within the armory or other designated secure storage area. The area itself should be climate-controlled, with the temperature and humidity within ranges that will maximize shelf life for all chemical agents and prevent weapon rusting.

All security equipment in storage, including ammunition and expendable supplies like grenades, must be clearly marked for identification, and inventories maintained for each category of equipment and supplies. These inventories must be reviewed at least monthly to assess the condition of the equipment and expiration dates of any expendable items like gas grenades and cartridges. Ammunition, tear gas, and other items that can leak or lose effectiveness because of aging must be replaced as needed, and the outdated items may be used for training.

Issue records must be maintained, noting to whom each item of security equipment is issued, or in the case of weapons maintained in towers, which post the weapon is on. These records are necessary to establish responsibility and accountability for the use of this equipment.

Except as otherwise provided by state law, personal weapons should not be used for official purposes, nor should employees use non-agency ammunition. In certain instances where employees live in agency housing near the institution, personal staff weapons and ammunition may be stored in the armory, but they should be in a separate area of the armory, under lock and key. This will prevent inadvertent issue during a crisis.

In many locations, a separate armory officer is identified for the purpose of maintaining the weapons program; in some, the armorer and locksmith functions are combined in one position. In any event, all weapons should be subject to a regular maintenance program that ensures that they are cleaned, fired regularly, and repaired as necessary.

## Loading and Unloading Areas

Safe firearms handling is a constant concern in a correctional institution. Since loading and unloading a weapon are inherently risky activities, most institutions have a specific area designated for these functions. This area is commonly a large barrel or other container full of sand, into which the barrel of the weapon is pointed when it is being loaded and unloaded. These areas are ordinarily located near entrances where weapons are unloaded before being secured, and are intended for use by both institutional personnel and visiting law enforcement officers.

## Armed Supervision

To reduce the risk of firearms falling into inmate hands, correctional officers who are in contact with inmates must not carry any weapons. Employees who use firearms while transporting or supervising inmates must be trained in the handling and use of these weapons, and safe techniques for inmate supervision.

If inmates require armed supervision when beyond the institutional perimeter, they ordinarily are assigned to jobs in the prison. However, if such inmates must work outside, great care must be taken to place them away from any armed officers. In

supervising work crews, armed staff should arrive before the inmates and remain until after they leave. Officers carrying firearms while transporting inmates outside the facility must be separated from them either by being located in a separate, secure compartment, or by riding in vehicles preceding or following the inmate vehicle.

## Documentation on Use

Whenever firearms are discharged or chemical agents used, officers must document exactly what happened. The report describing the incident must list the staff and inmates involved, the actions that caused the weapon use, and the person who authorized the action, if advance approval was obtained.

## When to Use Deadly Force

Staff should abide by specific agency policy in using deadly force, but in general, firearms should be used only when other means fail, and then only if less extreme measures will not serve the same purpose.

In most jurisdictions, an officer may fire under the following circumstances:

• At an inmate or other person carrying a weapon or attempting to obtain a weapon in order to harm others
• At an inmate or other person whom the officer has seen kill or seriously injure any person (whether or not a weapon is used) and who refuses to halt when ordered
• At an escaping inmate who cannot be stopped by nonlethal measures
• To protect equipment or vital property
• Mass fire should be used only as a last resort during escapes or serious assaults.

Staff should shout a clear warning before shooting, if time permits. Warning shots may be required by some agencies, and should be fired as long as there is no reasonable likelihood of serious injury or death to innocent people. If circumstances require a staff member to shoot an inmate, the fire should be aimed to wound and disable, rather than to kill.

Nondeadly ammunition can be used to control some violent situations. These include wooden or rubber bullets for shotguns, "beanbag" rounds for handguns, and other specialty cartridges. However, staff using them should be aware that even these rounds may be deadly at close range.

Firearms should be used inside the perimeter only as a last resort. Within the enclosed institution there may be staff or uninvolved inmates who could be exposed to direct gunfire or dangerous ricochets. Therefore, officers must exercise extreme caution when firing at targets within the security area.

Just as important is the concern for public safety when fire is directed at an escaping inmate outside the perimeter. Many institutions are located in urban areas, or have staff housing or other occupied buildings nearby. Tower or patrol staff must be particularly careful that their fire does not needlessly endanger innocent third parties.

## Use of Sharpshooters

The use of sharpshooters is a special case for deadly force situations. Only those staff who are properly trained and qualified on the specific weapon involved should be permitted to draw and use any sharpshooting weapons. Most institutions have a system set up for ensuring that only qualified staff draw and use these weapons.

These individuals must not only be thoroughly trained in the use of this equipment and experienced on the specific weapon they will use, but carefully briefed on the "rules of engagement" under which they may fire. In many cases, precise fire is only authorized upon the specific orders of a supervisor. In others, the shooter may be pre-authorized to fire if specific acts take place, such as a threatening act taken against a hostage. These conditions should be spelled out in advance, to the extent possible, and then additional briefing information provided at the time of a specific incident.

## Firearms Training

All personnel authorized to use firearms must receive appropriate training that covers the use, safety, care, and limits on the use of firearms. They must demonstrate proficiency in the use of institutional firearms on at least an annual basis, and the records of these qualification tests should be retained by the institution. Furthermore, each facility should have a system for assigning only these properly qualified staff to armed posts. As with so many other areas of practical corrections, safe firearms handling and use is best taught in a hands-on environment. However, there are a number of basic principles that can be reviewed here.

The first rule of handling weapons should be that all weapons should be treated as if they are loaded. Many lives have been lost because a loaded gun was believed to have been empty.

In addition to the presumption that all weapons are loaded, all firearms should be kept pointed in a safe direction, that is, away from other people. Weapons should never be pointed deliberately at anything other than the intended target. This rule is particularly true when loading and unloading a weapon, a time when, with some weapons, the action must be cycled. Weapons on post should be loaded; pistols should be carried in holsters and removed only for inspection or firing. Weapons in storage should always be unloaded.

# The first rule of handling weapons should be that all weapons should be treated as if they are loaded.

Officers should keep their fingers away from the trigger on a weapon until they are ready to fire. If a finger is on the trigger, an officer's reflex may cause a firearm to discharge accidentally, especially a firearm not equipped with a mechanical safety device.

## Firing Positions

The following information is intended as a general guide for firing certain categories of firearms. Specific training in weapons use is provided by the institution, and these firing positions may be taught somewhat differently from state to state. Actual aiming depends on the type of sight on the weapon: open, peep, laser, or telescopic.

### Rifle

There are four basic firing positions used for rifle fire.

*Standing.* Stand at a 45-degree angle to the right, with feet spread one to two feet apart and body erect and well balanced. Place the left elbow under the rifle, grasping it in front of the balance with the left hand, and resting the rifle on the palm of the left hand. Firmly hold the butt of the rifle high upon the right shoulder, with the right elbow approximately level with the shoulder. Press the right cheek against the stock and as far forward as comfortably possible.

*Kneeling.* Kneel on the right knee, supporting the body with the bent left leg. The right knee should point along the line of fire approximately at the target. The point of the left elbow should be over the left knee. Lean forward.

*Sitting.* There are several variations to the sitting position and every officer must find the one that is most comfortable and steady. Sitting at an angle to the intended target, and with legs spread comfortably at rest, lean forward and place each elbow on a knee, taking aim from that braced position.

*Prone.* Lying face down approximately 45 degrees with the line of fire, spread the legs wide apart and turn the heels inward. Flatten the stomach close to the ground, and place the point of the left elbow to the front and well to the right under the rifle. Raise the right shoulder, and with the right hand on the butt, place the rifle against the right shoulder and flatten it

out again. Position the right cheek snugly against the stock, grasping the small of the stock with the right hand and keeping the thumb along the stock, not across it. Extend the elbow and, drawing the body back, position the chest and body as close to the ground as possible. The left elbow should be directly under the gun. Extend the right elbow to raise the muzzle and bring the elbow in to lower it. In this position, the body will absorb the recoil.

### Shotguns

The intimidation value of a shotgun is often enough to deter even the most hardened inmates. In many cases, just the appearance of a shotgun on the scene will be enough to disperse a group of rioters. In other cases, a warning shot will have the same effect.

Although all of the positions described for rifle fire can be applied to a shotgun, ordinarily these weapons are fired from a standing position. In actual fire, however, the shotgun is used somewhat differently than a rifle. Rather than aiming for a specific point, this weapon is capable of hitting a wider area with multiple, smaller shot pellets. A particularly valuable firing strategy is to aim the weapon at the floor or ground, which will further spread the shot pattern and have the effect of striking more rioters. This also keeps the shot pattern low, reducing the chances of serious injuries.

One of the other keys to the proper use of the shotgun is selecting the correct ammunition. In the past, OO buckshot and other large shot sizes have been issued in institutions, and when fired, have caused serious injuries and death. If the intended purpose of weapons use is to disable, then using large shot sizes is inconsistent with that goal. As a result, many institutions have shifted their shotgun ammunition use toward smaller bird shot sizes that can disable inmates, but are less likely to kill them or harm bystanders hit by large ricocheting shot pellets.

### Handguns

Handguns are the third major category of weapon used by correctional staff. They are less accurate at a distance than rifles, less powerful than shotguns, but have the clear advantage of easy portability and concealability for escort work. Their use in tower or patrol operations is generally as a backup weapon.

The following general information is provided to give a picture of how pistols should be handled and used:

*Grip.* Grasp the butt so that the crotch of the thumb and forefinger are well up toward the hammer. Curl the second, third, and fourth fingers firmly (but not too tightly) around the butt of the gun. Lay the thumb up along the frame, parallel to the barrel. Lay the forefinger along and outside the trigger guard, so it is ready to pull the trigger instantly.

## *The intimidation value of a shotgun is often enough to deter even the most hardened inmates.*

*Stance.* The recommended position is comfortable and relaxed, and usually means facing the target at a 45-degree angle. Spread the feet 12 to 20 inches apart, the body erect and weight resting evenly on hips and feet; keep the back straight and the shoulders square, with the head held erect. Raise the right arm level with the shoulder, slightly bending the elbow. Turn the head, still held erect, to the right.

*Trigger Squeeze.* There usually is considerable slack to be taken up in pulling a trigger before the gun actually fires. While aiming, exert a steady backward pressure on the trigger to take up slack, continuing a steady pressure until the gun fires. Trigger snapping, or a quick hard jerk on the trigger, accounts for more poor shots than any other factor.

## Gas

In a riot situation, other, less forceful methods may not restore order; in those cases, the warden or designated senior officer may, after reviewing the situation, authorize staff to use tear gas or smoke compounds.

Gas may be used, within agency policy, under the following general conditions:

- To prevent serious injury or loss of life
- To prevent or suppress escalating riots or disturbances
- To prevent extensive, willful destruction of property

Tear gas operates by creating not only tears, but difficulty in breathing, stinging sensations, and other physical effects that disorient or disable inmates. Once secured or subdued, individuals exposed to tear gas should be permitted to wash and then be examined by a health care employee as soon as practical after exposure. They also should be monitored until no effects remain.

Gas may be deployed in several ways. The most common are the grenade and the 1.5" (37 mm) gas gun. Both can be used to spread gas in a relatively controlled manner in specific areas. Different types of grenades and gas gun cartridges are available, from blast dispersion types for a near-range problem, to long-range projectiles that can be fired over, or even through, barricades at a distance. Many of these

munitions have burning components and should be used with caution where a fire hazard may exist.

There are several additional methods of dispersing gas. These methods include aerosol dispensers, ranging in size from a hand-held unit for use in a cell to fire extinguisher-size containers for larger areas. There are devices that use the exhaust of a small gasoline engine to heat and propel the gas into large areas. There also are fixed placement gas systems that are sometimes seen in dining areas and other locations where large numbers of inmates may gather.

Smoke compounds are also available in the more common types of munitions, which can be used to confuse rioters, or to supplement and simulate gas. Smoke munitions should be as carefully controlled as gas, and should be authorized by the same level of official as gas use.

Staff should receive specific training in the use of gas guns, grenades, and other devices before being permitted to use them. Used in the wrong way, or the wrong circumstances, these munitions can be just as deadly as a standard firearm.

Officers using riot control gases should be taught, at a minimum, the following subjects and skills:

- The agency policy on the employment of riot control gases
- Characteristics of specific gases
- Squad organization and the use of gas
- Tactical deployment of gas
- Individual protection and first aid procedures for all people who have contact with gas
- The use and upkeep of gas munitions and equipment

Special safety precautions must be observed when using gas and smoke munitions and projections devices:

- All weapons and munitions must be handled with caution to prevent accidental firing and resulting harm to personnel or damage to property; they should never be aimed at a person.
- Safety pins must never be removed from grenades until officers are ready to throw them; employees must know the delay period for each specific type of grenade.
- Grenades must be thrown immediately after the safety grip is released.
- Safety rings must never be used for carrying grenades, or to hang grenades from pegs or hooks.

## Use of Restraints and Force

Force may be used to control inmates, but it must be in proportion to the threat posed by the inmate or inmates involved, and also follow any statutory procedures that apply. Justifiable circumstances often include self-defense, protection of others or property,

or to prevent escapes. In no case is physical force justifiable as punishment. When force is used, the incident must be thoroughly documented, and a full report sent to supervisors for review.

ACA standards limit the use of physical force to instances of justifiable self-defense, protection of others, protection of property, and prevention of escapes, as a last resort, and in any other situation approved by law.

Restraint equipment is a protective and precautionary measure to prevent assaults, prevent escapes during inmate transfers, serve medical purposes at the direction of a medical staff member, prevent inmate self-injury, or prevent damage to property. Restraints are never applied longer than is absolutely necessary.

Types of restraining devices may include:

- Swivel non-locking handcuffs
- Belly chains
- "Black boxes"
- Ankle shackles
- Restraining belts
- Plastic flex-tie handcuffs
- Thumb cuffs
- Strait jackets
- Restraining sheets
- Restraining straps

Restraint use involves the following general principles:

- Handcuffing inmates does not render them harmless—inmates can still assault an officer or attempt to escape.
- Maximum-security, segregated, or detained inmates must be restrained before moving them out of their cells.
- For high-risk cases, handcuffs may be applied from behind; extra restraints like "belly chains" and "black boxes" may be applied when indicated by agency or institutional policy.
- Restraints should be checked periodically by officers transporting inmates.
- Inmates ordinarily should not be secured to any motionless object, including an automobile; they should never be secured to a moving vehicle.
- Officers must be alert in applying or removing restraints; that is the time when they are most vulnerable.

## Unarmed Self-Defense

Unarmed self-defense techniques for staff can be useful in the correctional setting; they involve using self-protection moves that require no special equipment. Officers may employ basic defense holds if threatened or assaulted by an inmate, but in no case may physical force be used as punishment. The following techniques are listed to show the variety of self-defense maneuvers available to trained staff:

- Come-alongs
- Breaks for choke holds

- Defensive moves against weapons, such as knives and clubs
- Defensive moves against swings to the head and body
- Defensive moves against the pinning of the arms

As in using firearms, constant practice and supervision in unarmed defense are necessary to maintain proficiency in the techniques. In addition to the many manuals and visual aids available, employees also need to watch qualified instructors demonstrate the holds, and then practice the movements under supervision.

## Emergency Response Teams

Almost all institutions provide basic emergency response training to all staff, including squad formations and tactics. However, many institutions have a special emergency response team, which is trained specifically to respond to institutional crises such as fights, riots, forced cell moves, or hostage situations.

These employees are almost always selected according to written criteria and receive additional training in squad tactics, use of special weapons, and other emergency reaction strategies. These staff may be on call throughout the day by radio, and may even carry paging equipment when off duty so they can be quickly recalled to the institution during nonduty hours.

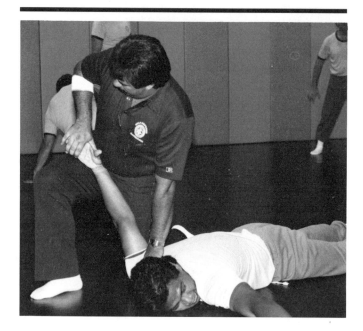

Other locations take the approach that since all correctional workers are trained in emergency response tactics, a special team is not needed. The advantage to this approach is that it is less expensive, and also that at any given time, a response team can be assembled. The disadvantage is that the specific group assembled for a given crisis may never have worked together before, and may not be as efficient.

There is no single best solution to this problem, and local administrators choose the most practical response team strategy for their institution based on available staff and other factors. For instance, in a camp setting, there is a low probability of ever needing a response team at all, so there would be little need to provide training and ongoing support to a special response team; regular staff training is sufficient. However, in a high-security institution where there are a relatively large number of forced cell moves and other confrontational incidents, a trained, well-disciplined team that works together regularly can be a tremendous asset.

## Forced Cell Moves

Unarmed techniques may also involve the methods used to remove inmates who refuse to come out of their cells and must be forcibly restrained and taken to a locked unit. All forced moves of this type should be directed by a supervisory staff member, and a full report filed on each such incident.

The staff assigned to a forced cell move should be properly equipped for their personal safety. Jumpsuits, helmets, defensive shields, and even bulletproof or penetration-resistant vests should be provided.

## ACA Firearms Standards

ACA standards regarding firearms include the following provisions:
- Weapons are subject to stringent safety regulations and inspections.
- Except in emergency situations, officers carrying firearms are assigned only to watchtowers, gun walks, mobile patrols, or other positions inaccessible to inmates.
- Officers supervising inmates outside the institution perimeter follow procedures that ensure the security of weapons.
- Officers are instructed to use deadly force only after other actions have been tried, and were ineffective, unless the officer believes that a person's life or institutional security is immediately threatened.
- Officers on duty use only firearms issued by the institution, and use them only when directed by the warden/superintendent or officer in charge.

Many institutions now use a coordinated move strategy that greatly simplifies the process of subduing, restraining, and removing a rebellious inmate from a small cell. This involves each staff member being assigned a specific limb to subdue or function to perform (such as applying leg irons or handcuffs or pinning the inmate with a shield). In the confusion of a fight with an inmate, this strategy can prevent several people grabbing for one of the inmate's arms and no one restraining the other arm, or no one grabbing the inmate's legs, allowing the inmate to kick and injure staff unnecessarily. With each staff member on the team assigned a specific role, the move can proceed quickly and efficiently, with a minimum of injury to staff or the inmate.

If possible, the forced move itself should be video taped, to use as evidence against the inmate if a criminal prosecution results. In many institutions that use the video-taping strategy, the mere presence of a camera deters the inmate from any violent action. The presence of a camera also is a reminder to staff to be totally professional in their actions.

## Summary

Correctional officers must know the correct procedures for using firearms, gas, and physical force, and clearly understand who may authorize it. This chapter should be regarded only as a general introduction to this topic. Individuals must develop the necessary firearms, gas, and self-defense skills through training and practice.

*APPLICABLE ACA STANDARDS*

Security and Control: 3-4166 and 3-4191 to 3-4197
Training and Development: 3-4086 to 3-4089

# 7

# Emergency Plans and Procedures

Day-to-day application of such sound correctional practices as inmate accountability, security inspections, and tool and key control contributes greatly to an institution's security. But overcrowding, inmate idleness, understaffing, severe budget constraints, and even natural disasters can create situations that lead to disruptions of institutional routines. In those moments, the existence of a well-developed set of institutional emergency plans will pay tremendous dividends.

ACA standards require that institutions have written plans to be followed in situations that threaten institutional security. These plans—including but not limited to riots, mass food strikes, disturbances, and hostage taking—should be available to all institutional personnel, and reviewed and updated at least annually. The plans must include notification of law enforcement agencies about the emergency, temporary measures pending the arrival of top officials, actual riot control, instructions for separating and temporarily housing ringleaders, and steps for resuming normal operations.

The plans developed for each institution will be unique to that facility. The physical plant, staffing patterns, and even statutory requirements in which it operates determine the specific way a plan is developed. However, there are a number of general principles common to all emergency plans.

## Emergency Plan Structure

Each institution should have a complete set of emergency plans that include strategies for dealing with at least the following situations:

- Riots
- Escapes
- Fires
- Bombs
- Hostage situations
- Civil disturbances
- Inmate work/food strikes
- Fog/reduced visibility
- Employee job actions
- Natural disasters
- Emergency staff recalls

Each problem situation should be the subject of a separate plan. Each plan should include a set of general guidelines for detecting the signs of impending problems and preventing the problems, and then provide an overall structure for developing a specific response to each individual crisis. The plan should at least generally identify the major issues that will have to be dealt with and describe possible response options, as well as hard content like vital telephone numbers and locations. Plans must be developed and refined specifically for each institution; a single plan for all facilities in an agency is not practical.

In addition to the specific content of each plan, a formal cover sheet should be included in each, with the warden's signature, indicating plan approval. Regular high-level review of all plans is a necessity; an administrative review should be conducted not less than once a year as an integral part of the emergency plan system, to update the plan as policies, staffing, and institutional construction change.

These plans ordinarily are maintained in loose-leaf binders so that changes and updates can be made easily. With the increasing use of word processors, the plans can be easily revised and reissued each year at the time of the annual review.

The contents of the emergency plans should be

covered in initial and refresher training, and staff must be required to review all plans at least annually so that they are familiar with their provisions. This is often done through a checkout system. The emergency plan review system should also require staff to sign off on a review documentation sheet when they review each plan.

This training and review process is important because there is no way of predicting who will be on duty in a critical post in a time of crisis. A senior officer may be in an acting supervisor's position, a department head may be acting as an associate warden—each of these individuals and staff at every other level need to know the overall plan for response.

## Common Emergency Plan Information

Although each agency's emergency plan differs, most contain at least the following basic information:

- A definition of the emergency situation the plan is meant to deal with
- Key indicators of potential problems in that area
- Preventive steps to take, if possible; this may be the most important element in many plans, like those for riots and escapes
- A notification point for reporting the problem
- Immediate operational steps to take to secure the institution
- The chain of command during nonduty hours
- The telephone numbers and identity of key officials to be notified
- The sequence of notification
- People authorized to call in additional staff
- People authorized to notify outside authorities
- The location of a command center for emergency operational control
- Secondary operational steps to take to resolve the situation

*Emergency plans must include notification of law enforcement agencies about the emergency, temporary measures pending the arrival of top officials, actual riot control, instructions for separating and temporarily housing ringleaders, and steps for resuming normal operations.*

- The person authorized to notify the media and release information
- Current telephone numbers for all staff and key outside parties, such as the state police
- A statement containing the agency's hostage policy

For situations like riots, escapes, and other preventable incidents, each emergency plan should emphasize signs of tension and unusual circumstances in the institution, and other contributing factors that staff can be aware of that often telegraph a major impending problem. In addition, the plans should emphasize preventive measures that can be taken when these signs are in evidence.

For many emergencies, joint training with other agencies on emergency plan implementation can be a tremendous benefit. To effectively deal with a riot or fire, for instance, it is important to have employee emergency plan training in cooperation with local fire fighters or state police. This joint training should include drills during which the agencies involved participate in simulated responses to institutional emergencies. This is a valuable training strategy, and also develops closer cooperation and understanding among the various agencies involved in emergency responses to institutional crises.

All plans should include information on media access and notification in all relevant emergency plans, because any major disturbance in a correctional institution attracts news media attention. In fact, such news media involvement often is the first thing demanded by inmates during a crisis. All relevant plans should include specific information about media contacts by staff, establishment of a briefing area, and other important details. An official spokesperson should be identified. Media representatives should not be involved in any emergency activities.

## Preparedness Checklists

In addition to regular training, some agencies have adopted a regular emergency preparedness checklist strategy. Checklists might include, but not necessarily be limited to, regular reviews of the following areas or items:

- Firearms and ammunition; weapons must be operable and ammunition fresh
- Gas munitions and equipment; gas supplies should be current, but old gas may be used for training purposes
- Emergency lighting equipment and facilities, including those available from outside agencies
- Fire-fighting equipment and personnel; Air-pacs should be available for immediate response to smoke-filled areas
- Shut-off valves for water, electricity, gas, heat, and ventilation
- Emergency entrances to all buildings
- Emergency key systems and their use
- A general alarm system
- Availability of emergency personnel, including current telephone lists and call-up systems
- Amplifiers, public address systems, and other communication equipment
- Location and secure storage of critical supplies and equipment, especially those that can be burned or used as weapons, such as gasoline, poisons, ladders, and torches
- Portable welding equipment, bolt cutters, and other specialized response equipment
- Current floor plans of all parts of the institution

## Security Inspections

Some physical features of the institution have a bearing on emergency responses to fires, escapes, riots, and other crisis situations. A regular security inspection program, as described elsewhere in this guide, should ensure that they are operating as intended. It is particularly critical to ensure the full operating status of:

- Emergency doors
- Locking devices
- Functioning of sallyports in key areas
- Emergency power systems
- Fire-fighting equipment
- Communication systems and alarms
- Specific plans

## Riots

Institutional disturbances may range from a minor outburst involving several inmates to a major riot involving the entire population, from a passive "sit-down" demonstration to large-scale, random destruction of life and property. Disturbances can start

with inmates' spontaneous reactions to a stabbing, or they can be organized, calculated movements of mass resistance supported and assisted by outside groups or led by inmates using revolutionary tactics. They also may start as a result of a disturbance in another institution somewhere in the state's prison system or the country. Each type of disturbance requires different response tactics. Therefore, it is essential that the riot plan be sufficiently flexible to cover all possibilities, but contain specific tactical and administrative information that will help shape the proper response.

A well-written riot control plan provides administrators with sufficient response flexibility, and is clearly and concisely written so that it is easily understood by all. It ensures deployment of all personnel and equipment to the problem areas as quickly and efficiently as possible.

A well-developed plan will have basic content on the following elements:

• *Reporting.* The emergency plan should emphasize the need to report a disturbance immediately to a central location, usually the control center. This allows officials maximum time to isolate and bring the problem under control before it escalates and involves a greater area or more inmates.

• *Notification and call-up procedures.* Upon being notified of a disturbance, the control center officer should contact the shift supervisor. The plan should then specify prompt notification of staff on perimeter posts, front and rear entrances, the powerhouse, all areas where there are likely to be groups of inmates, and then administrative staff—the warden, associate warden, chief correctional supervisor, and others. If the shift supervisor cannot be contacted, the control center officer ordinarily is authorized to initiate these emergency notification procedures independently.

• *Intelligence gathering.* The plan should address the need to quickly gather information about the nature and scope of the disturbance, number of staff hostages (if any) and other key facts. If the situation continues, then an ongoing intelligence-gathering and analysis process must be in place.

• *Selection and assignment of officers for emergency squads.* The plan should clearly identify the categories of staff to be mustered for response action, how they are to be organized, and where they will be staged while awaiting action, as well as timekeeping and other administrative details.

• *Developing options for action.* The riot plan should include general information on the tactical options available for retaking the institution, from securing with a single, small area to the entire compound. While each crisis will differ, there is no doubt that similar principles can be employed in many riot situations. The plan should contain information on squad use, deployment of gas, utility controls, and other crowd and riot suppression activities. It also

should include an awareness of the importance of not overreacting to the crisis and creating even greater problems.

• *Notification of outside parties.* Specific authority to notify local law enforcement authorities should be contained in the plan; local utility companies may also have to be notified to assist staff in maintaining or cutting off utility service in the institution.

• *Use of outside organizations.* The plan should describe staff deployment methods, and provide that only trained correctional officers are assigned inside an institution during a disturbance, unless the situation is so serious as to require the police or National Guard to assist in providing additional coverage in retaking the facility. Outside law enforcement personnel and institutional staff who are untrained in riot control may be used to secure the perimeter, to control gates, or to supervise areas where they are unlikely to encounter inmates.

• *Curtailment of normal programs.* The plan must provide for a measured, nonpunitive response to small-scale incidents, so as to not alienate the majority of inmates, who may not be active participants, as is often the case.

---

# A well-written riot control plan provides administrators with sufficient response flexibility.

• *Selection and use of equipment, including firearms and gas.* The plan should provide for rapid issue of emergency equipment to staff only, including items such as riot helmets, batons, communication equipment, shotguns, gas and gas equipment, shields, emergency keys, cutting torches, wrenches, wrecking bars, ropes, and portable lights. This often is done by maintaining ready boxes of enough personal equipment to outfit one squad, and pre-prepared weapons kits that have a firearm, ammunition, and other necessary gear ready for issue from the armory.

• *Weapon and equipment accountability.* All equipment issued must be accounted for through a pre-prepared, positive identification system of some type. The confusion of a riot is no time to try to set up an accountability system.

• *Follow-up.* The riot plan must address not only the actual emergency and the retaking of the institution from a tactical point of view. It must at least consider the following pre- and post-riot considerations:

- Taking an official count of all inmates
- Accounting for all staff
- Ensuring due process for participants who may be prosecuted
- Securing evidence for subsequent prosecutions
- Evacuating unserviceable sections of the institution, as well as temporarily evacuating areas where gas has been used and decontamination is necessary
- Maintaining or resuming physical plant operations
- Revising dining schedules to serve meals in cells, or to serve smaller groups in the central dining area
- Assigning additional personnel to living quarters and dining rooms until the atmosphere in the institution returns to normal
- Conducting an extensive, thorough investigation

beginning with interviewing staff, ringleaders, and other participants
- Assisting staff or law enforcement personnel in preserving and/or photographing physical evidence or damaged areas, which may later be used as legal evidence
- Arranging for physical examinations and treatment and psychological care for staff, particularly former hostages
- Arranging for physical examinations and medical care for injured inmates
- Preparing a full report for the appropriate agency authority, summarizing the origins of the riot, the actual events, staff response, and the events in the aftermath

## Escapes

No matter how secure the institution, inmates will try to escape. During an escape attempt, officers must act quickly to stop the attempt and recapture the inmate. That is why a functional escape plan is vitally important for every institution. While the methods used by inmates in escape attempts vary, escape plans should contain the fundamental search and surveillance techniques that cover most situations.

A functional plan includes the following elements:

- *Definition*. A clear definition of what specifically constitutes an escape in the particular jurisdiction involved, as opposed to an inmate being "off-limits," "out of bounds," or some other lesser infraction.
- *Reporting an escape*. Staff in the institution must know who they should notify in the event they believe an inmate is missing. In most cases this is the control center.
- *Alerting the perimeter and gateposts*. As soon as an inmate is believed to be missing, the perimeter and gatepost staff should be notified, as well as any outlying patrol staff.
- *Securing the area*. The entire institution should be secured; inmates must return to their quarters.
- *Accountability*. The institution should be counted immediately, to determine the identity of missing inmates; in most cases, a picture card count will be needed, to verify the identity of those missing.
- *Notifying top staff*. The plan should specify the order in which top staff should be notified, usually starting with the warden.
- *Hostage information*. The plan should clearly state that no inmate

> *An institution's physical plant, staffing patterns, and even statutory requirements in which it operates determine the specific way an emergency plan is developed.*

with a hostage is to be released, and that no hostage has any authority.

• *Identifying key posts to continue to staff.* Some areas can be secured and their staff assigned to the escape hunt; others such as the powerhouse and food service must continue to operate; these positions should be identified in advance so no confusion results from removing staff from a critical post.

• *Establishment of a command center.* This area includes not only internal communications and command functions, but also communication with local and state law enforcement personnel assisting in the escape hunt.

• *Staff recall.* Using current lists of all employees and pre-established call-up procedures, off-duty employees should be called in.

• *Notifying local law enforcement.* This section of the plan should specify who is authorized to notify local law enforcement personnel of the escape, and by what means; it may also involve distribution of escape flyers.

• *Internal searches to apprehend hideouts.* The plan should specify internal search procedures to apprehend inmates who may be hiding out inside the facility, awaiting darkness, fog, or some other time when it may be more favorable to try to escape the secure compound.

• *Establishing outside escape posts.* The plan should establish fixed and roving escape posts, identify the

equipment that should go on each post, and describe the other procedures necessary to staff these posts, including issue of equipment.

• *Staff support on escape posts.* The regular relief, feeding, and checking of staff on remote posts must be provided for.

• *Strategies for apprehending and restraining escapees.* The plan should provide staff with clear guidance on actions they should and should not take when apprehending an escapee. At least two officers should be present to search escapees after they are captured; if only one officer captures an inmate, the inmate should stay "spread-eagle" on the ground until backup assistance arrives.

• *Notification of capture.* When inmates have been captured, the procedures must specify who will notify all law enforcement agencies, communities, and the media.

• *Interviews with escapees.* The plan must ensure that any interviews with escapees are done in a way that does not hamper the criminal prosecution of the escapee by compromising any constitutional rights.

## Fires

Fires in institutions can threaten hundreds of lives, endanger the facility and surrounding communities, and result in tremendous financial losses. Moreover, because of the confined quarters and crowded conditions of many institutions, fires can present an even greater danger than in an ordinary setting.

ACA standards provide a clear view of an effective fire prevention program, which includes, but is not limited to, the following elements:

- Adequate fire protection service from a combination of inside and outside sources
- Regular fire inspections and quarterly testing of equipment
- Annual inspection by local or state fire officials or other qualified people
- Fire protection equipment located appropriately throughout the institution, as required by the National Fire Protection Association's Life Safety Code
- A full-time crew of inmate fire fighters who meet custody standards and training levels necessary to cope with any type of fire in and around the institution
- Availability of fire-fighting equipment that includes, at a minimum, a modern fire truck complete with pressure pumps, tanks, and modern, portable extinguishers
- An automatic fire alarm and smoke detection system certified by an independent, qualified inspector; if the institution relies on a local fire department, the system may be connected directly
- Quarterly tests of all systems and annual certification by a state fire official
- A written evacuation plan for fires and other emergencies, certified by an outside inspector trained in the application of national fire safety codes

A well-developed fire plan incorporates the basic concepts in the ACA standards and has the following elements:

- *Prevention.* The first line of defense in any fire plan is an aggressive fire prevention and safety program.
- *Staff training.* Initial and refresher training should cover basic fire prevention and suppression topics, as well as the use of basic fire equipment; this should include institutional familiarization tours by local fire-fighting personnel.
- *Inmate information activities.* Inmates should be advised in orientation, unit meetings, and through other programs of the hazards of carelessly handling cigarettes, flammable materials, welding equipment, etc.
- *Control of flammable materials.* The proper control of hazardous substances is very important to preventing accidental and purposely set fires.
- *Notification.* The same sequence of notification as used for the riot plan may be employed in the fire plan; procedures for notifying local fire authorities should be specified.

- *Inmate fire crews.* The use of trained inmate fire fighters under officers' supervision can be an important factor in fighting an institutional fire; the procedures for their use should be clearly spelled out in the plan and these inmates should be housed together for quick response to a fire alarm.
- *Evacuation plans and routes.* Evacuation charts with clearly identified escape routes should be prominently posted; officers must be familiar with release and backup systems for inmates.
- *Escort procedures for outside fire fighters.* The plan should specify gate processing procedures for community fire-fighting crews and equipment, including search and escort procedures whenever trucks and other equipment are brought inside the institution.
- *Fire drills.* Quarterly drills should include evacuation of all inmates, except when there is clear and convincing evidence that institutional security would be jeopardized; in those instances, staff should walk through their roles in quarterly drills.
- *Post-fire care of inmates.* The plan should provide direction for moving and housing inmates, and for providing injured staff or inmates medical care and transportation to hospitals.
- *Post-fire investigation.* In the case of major fires, the institutional staff should preserve the fire scene to the degree possible, in order to enable trained investigators to properly determine the fire's origins.

## Bombs

Although some institutions, like a metropolitan jail, may have bomb threats relating to their perimeter, bombs inside the institution are more commonly a concern. However, sophisticated bombs smuggled in by a visitor or other third party are not the primary explosives problem inside a prison; inmates can easily fabricate bombs from match heads and other simple materials and bombs of that type are far more common. For that reason, staff need to be prepared to deal with these dangerous explosive devices.

The plan should emphasize proper reaction to bomb threats and actual bomb handling, and include the following elements:

*Telephone threats.* The plan should instruct switchboard and control center staff in particular, but all staff in general, on the procedures to follow and information to try to obtain if a bomb threat should be telephoned into the institution.

*Notification.* If a suspected bomb is discovered, the staff member should immediately secure the area and notify a supervisor.

*Movement of bombs.* Suspected bombs should never be moved.

*Evacuation.* The plan needs to emphasize "evacuating people not bombs." This point cannot be driven home too strongly, and it should be included in bold type and underlined in each copy of the bomb plan.

*Use of radios.* Bombs that are wired to explode may pick up enough electrical energy from nearby radio transmissions to be detonated; most bomb plans call for stopping all radio traffic until the device is deactivated or removed from the institution.

*Expert assistance.* Few institutions have staff with the expertise to safely examine and deactivate even the simplest explosive device; local law enforcement or military expertise should be arranged in advance, and the notification procedures contained in the bomb plan.

*Booby traps.* Inmates have set booby-trap bombs in various locations, severely injuring staff; employees conducting searches must be very careful to not disturb any potential bomb or trigger a booby-trap device, and to call for help immediately.

## Hostages

Inmates occasionally take hostages with the intent of trying to effect an escape or to gain some concession from the administration. Hostages are often taken in the course of a riot.

There is not total agreement on the issue of hostage negotiations versus retaking the hostages by

## *For many emergencies, joint training with other agencies on emergency plan implementation can be a tremendous benefit.*

force. Conventional wisdom generally holds that if the hostages can be quickly recovered by a tactical response, then that course of action should be taken. However, once some time has passed and the hostage takers have had a chance to become organized, the history of a great many prison hostage situations seems to point toward the wisdom of patient, fair negotiations to free hostages.

A typical hostage plan includes sections on the following:

*Hostage policy.* Hostage plans should clearly indicate that no one held hostage has any authority, and that no inmate will be released while holding anyone under duress. To do otherwise would encourage inmates to view every staff member as a potential avenue for escape, and no one would be safe. If all inmates understand that taking a hostage will not result in their release, the risk of this kind of incident is greatly reduced.

*Post orders.* In addition to being in the hostage plan itself, most institutions include a hostage statement in all emergency plans and the post orders of all perimeter and gatepost positions, as well as the control center. This is particularly necessary for the plans that relate to disturbances and escapes, although any emergency could conceivably be used as a diversion for a hostage-type escape, and thus all plans should contain this information.

*Securing the area.* This section of the plan should ensure that staff take the proper precautions to secure the area in which the hostages are being held, to prevent additional inmates from joining or otherwise reinforcing the hostage takers by bringing weapons or supplies.

*Identifying the hostages.* As quickly as possible, the staff in charge of the incident need to know who the hostages are, if they have any special health problems, and other vital details.

*Identifying the hostage takers.* The identity of the hostage takers is often critical to successful management of a hostage incident in a prison. Special details about their cases, background, or behavioral characteristics can be used in negotiations and in briefing the response teams that may be called on to free the hostages by force.

*Notification of nonprison officials, hostage families, media, and other agencies.* The plan should identify the people responsible for notifying noninstitutional parties, starting with the appropriate law enforcement agencies and the hostages' family members.

*Establishing negotiations.* Once it is apparent that the hostages cannot be safely retrieved at the onset of an incident, then the plan should provide for the option of negotiating for their release. The area of hostage negotiations is quite complex, but basically this plan should include the assignment of trained hostage negotiators who are familiar with the institution or correctional operations, but who are not authority figures. The media and third parties should not be part of the negotiations.

*Profiling the hostage takers.* The facility should attempt to construct a psychological profile of the hostage takers, for use by the negotiators.

*Concessions.* In general, no substantial concessions are ever made in hostage negotiations. Minor exchanges of photographs or notes by hostages, for some equally minor favor, can be the basis for larger exchanges later, like the release of some hostages for turning on the water again. However, under no circumstance can a major concession like release of the hostage takers ever be part of the negotiations.

*Prosecution policy.* The issue of prosecution often comes up in the negotiations. Agency policy usually states that there will be full prosecution for all crimes committed during the course of a hostage incident, and prosecutors for that jurisdiction usually take that position also.

*Care of hostages after release.* The plan should provide for the immediate, positive identification of all released hostages, their medical examination, and any necessary follow-up psychological or psychiatric care.

*Hostage family issues.* Whenever possible, the

families of hostages should receive special information briefings in a private area where they can remain free from harassment by the media and other third parties throughout the crisis. A ranking official should be available periodically to brief them, and other staff like chaplains or psychologists can assist them as they wait for the release of their loved ones.

## Civil Disturbances

In rare occasions, institutional operations are disrupted by civil disturbances in the vicinity of the facility. This may be deliberate, in the case of a radical group trying to disrupt institutional operations, or it may be a side effect of another local problem unrelated to the prison.

The institution's plan for these occasions should include the following points:

*Maintaining staff coverage.* If the disturbance disrupts staff access to the institution, then the plan should outline alternate coverage for key security posts, and vital services like utilities and food service.

*Outside law enforcement liaison.* The plan should include information on notification, liaison personnel, joint command centers, and jurisdictional issues.

*Intrusion prevention.* Clear information should be provided on blockading or barricading the institutional property; methods for preventing unauthorized access to the institutional property; deterring, repelling, or apprehending intruders; and other issues.

*Limits of staff authority.* In the event that a civil disturbance results in unauthorized entry of civilians on the institutional property or overt acts against institutional property, the plan should clearly state whether institutional employees have power of arrest or detention.

*Monitoring inmate reaction.* Staff should be alert to spontaneous, disruptive inmate reactions to an outside disturbance, as well as the possibility of a coordinated effort between outside agitators and inmates.

## Inmate Work/Food Strike

Inmates sometimes stage food or work strikes as a form of protest against institutional conditions, or in reaction to outside agitation or events. Each institution should have a plan that ensures that essential services are maintained in the face of these disruptive events.

Typical plans for food and work strikes include these factors:

*Prevention.* The signs of these disruptive acts are often similar to those of an impending riot.

*Identification of leaders and agitators.* Identifying inmates who may be trying to agitate a strike (by circulating among groups, getting signatures on

petitions, and other actions). Once a strike is under way, staff should be alert to the inmates who actively advocate its continuance. Removing the leaders from the general population is a key step to strike management.

*Determination of actual grievances.* There should be options in the plan for gaining credible information from inmates about the reason for the strike. This may be through interviews, surveys, or unit meetings, but they should focus on the broadest possible range of sources, not just the inmate leaders.

*Curtailment of normal programs.* The plan must provide for a measured, nonpunitive response, so as to not alienate the majority of inmates, who may not be active supporters, but who feel pressured to go along with a few verbal, aggressive agitators.

*Alternate food service operations.* In the event a work stoppage involves food service workers, staff must arrange alternate coverage in the food preparation area, and have plans ready for serving meals to inmates in smaller groups, on extended schedules, or via sack meals in their cells. In some prisons, the contingency plan could provide for the use of minimum-security camp inmates in meal preparation, but care should be taken that they do not come in contact with the higher security strikers.

## Fog/Reduced Visibility

Each institution should have a reduced visibility plan that ensures inmates do not have an opportunity to use fog or other weather conditions to cover an escape. This plan should state:

• *Supervisory responsibility.* Identify the supervisor responsible for making the decision to implement the plan.

• *Criteria for decision making.* Give some general criteria for visibility that will be used to make that decision.

• *Special posts.* Identify any additional posts that should be staffed until visibility improves.

• *Special precautions indicated.* Describe any internal movement restrictions that will be in place, such as escorted movement, special counts, or curtailment of work assignments.

## Employee Job Action

Although most agencies do not face the likelihood of an employee job action, because of laws prohibiting public employee strikes, there should be some

## All emergency plans should include information on media access and notification because any major disturbance in a correctional institution attracts news media attention.

contingency plan for this kind of crisis. While the most common such action might be a "blue flu" or mass sick call, a full work stoppage by staff is not totally beyond the realm of possibility.

A contingency plan for this kind of situation involves developing options in these areas:

*Assessment of the nature of the action.* Administrative staff should attempt at the earliest possible moment to learn the type of job action planned, how extensive it might be, and how long it might last. This information will assist in planning to bring in workers from other government agencies, including the state police or National Guard. It will also form the basis for beginning to develop a response strategy with the leaders of the job action.

• *Notification of other agencies.* Once a job action of this type is clearly about to occur, or is under way, the plan should identify the responsible authority who will notify other government agencies, as well as the media. As the employees participating in the action may well have already notified the media, a public information structure should also be put in place.

• *Assignment of alternate post coverage.* To ensure that vital institution functions are continued, the plan should identify key posts to keep active, and a priority listing of those areas that can be shut down for the duration of the job action. In addition, supervisory and management staff, and any other employees who are not members of the bargaining unit who report for work, should be ready for assignment to these critical posts. This part of the plan should also provide for timekeeping and relief of staff.

• *Curtailment of inmate services.* To the degree possible, inmate activities should not be curtailed, unless they involve security risks. In some instances, a limited "lockdown" may be necessary in the housing units to keep other areas like food service in operation.

• *Communications with inmates.* In order to prevent any undue inmate reaction to the job action, managerial staff should keep inmates advised of the steps being taken to continue near-normal operations, and to restore the institution to normal functioning as soon as possible. Staff on duty should be alert to the possibility of inmate agitators taking advantage of this situation to stir up the inmate population as well.

• *Process for returning to normal operation.* As staff return to work there should be a strategy for reactivating posts and programs that have been curtailed by the job action. This ordinarily would include expanding food service operations to normal, and carefully restoring work, recreation, education, and other programs as more employees are available for the proper level of supervision.

## Disasters

While unlikely, the threat of disasters like tornadoes, floods, a nearby train wreck with a hazardous material release, and other events must be anticipated in the institution's contingency planning process. These plans differ greatly according to the facility's location; it is unlikely that an institution in Oregon will experience a tornado, or that a facility in an arid part of the country would experience a flood. However, the problems presented by most disasters are similar in certain respects, and a general plan can help staff think about how they would deal with the following issues:

• *Notification of impending disaster.* Most institutions can monitor any local emergency radio or weather networks that would signal a coming severe storm or a nearby major accident that might affect institutional operations. In other areas, contacts with local law enforcement and civil defense personnel can ensure that the institution will be warned as soon as possible of an impending problem. These warnings are usually received in the institution's control center.

• *Agency notification.* In most cases, only one institution in an agency would be affected by a severe storm, flood, or other disaster. The parent agency should be notified at once, so that assistance from other institutions and state agencies can be coordinated.

• *Staff notification.* As soon as the institution is notified, supervisory staff on duty and other officials should be advised. It may also be advisable to notify staff on posts, and even to begin an advance staff recall, so that enough employees are available to supervise an evacuation or other unusual response to the crisis.

• *Inmate communications.* Once the impending crisis is thought to have an effect on the institution, the inmate population should be advised and told of the response, if any, that will be required of them. In most cases, no dramatic inmate movement will be involved, but there may be a curtailment of activities; inmates should be told why, how long it may last,

and what they can expect to receive in the way of activities and privileges in the meantime. As in many other crisis situations, staff should carefully observe the population for signs of agitators and others who would take advantage of this situation.

• *Evacuation procedures.* The emergency plan should contain a set of options for evacuation of selected portions of the institution, as well as the entire facility, if necessary. This part of the plan entails supervision, restraints, transportation, outside assistance, and liaison with other institutions if a mass transfer is needed.

• *Supply issues.* If an extended emergency prevented delivery of perishable food items and other critical supply items, the plan should cover contingencies for delivery.

• *Staff housing and meals.* In the event staff are stranded in the institution, or enough staff cannot report for duty and employees must be held over, then accommodations must be available for them.

• *Utilities.* Continuation of key utilities will be a priority, if only to ensure that security, fire safety, and sanitation systems are available. Key staff and other information items on this subject should be a part of the plan.

• *Assistance from other agencies.* In addition to notification of the impact a crisis may be having on the institution, it may be necessary to call on other agencies like the National Guard for support. The contact points and telephone numbers for these agencies should be in the plan.

## Emergency Recall Plan

The staff recall plan can be a separate plan, or a subsection of other emergency plans. This is basically a local system for quickly notifying off-duty staff that they are needed at the institution for some emergency.

The "pyramid" style of telephone call notification speeds up staff call-ups in emergencies. This is a structured call-up system that specifies certain employees who are called first, and they, in turn, call several other specified employees, who themselves call several others. This method considerably speeds up telephone notifications in a crisis, and does not unduly burden any one staff member with a large number of calls.

In recent years, new technologies have become available that can be used to speed this process. One in particular allows for a computer equipped with a specific accessory board to be connected to a telephone line, and to automatically make a sequence of calls, telling those who answer the telephone that the institution is calling in all employees.

## Summary

Effective emergency procedures are fundamental to all institutions. They cover the general steps to be taken before, during, and following institutional crises. The possibility of emergencies occurring means that officers must continually review the emergency response plans and practice the necessary emergency skills.

For more comprehensive information, see ACA's *Guidelines for the Development of a Security Program* and *Riots and Disturbances in Correctional Institutions.*

*APPLICABLE ACA STANDARDS*

Physical Plant: 3-4206, 3-4209, 3-4120, 3-4121, and 3-4127

Safety and Emergency Procedures: 3-4121 and 3-4199 to 3-4210

Security and Control: 3-4205 and 3-4211 to 3-4213

# 8

# Food Service

Food service operations have the challenging mission of providing inmates with three meals a day, 365 days a year, without fail. In addition, the meals must be nutritious, tasty, attractive, and produced under sanitary conditions, at reasonable costs.

Food service operations have an enormous effect on inmate morale and health. Many work and food strikes, and even riots, started with inmate complaints about food. To the degree that institution staff can make sure that the meals served are nutritious, appealing in appearance, and sufficiently varied, they will be ensuring that this major management variable will not create unnecessary problems.

In some locations, a contract with a private food service company is used to provide food services. Even when private parties are involved, however, the basic principles described in this chapter still apply. Some of the information contained in this chapter is not strictly related to correctional supervision. Additional detail is included because food service is such an important part of institution life, and because correctional staff are often assigned to work in the kitchen to supervise the general area.

## Food Service Organization

Most correctional institutions in the United States have extensive food service facilities and equipment. The most common method used to provide meals to inmates is a modified cafeteria system. Architectural designs and the arrangement of equipment vary from facility to facility, but a food line, with individuals selecting quantities of most items, is the most practical way of serving large numbers of inmates.

ACA standards provide a general picture of how a

well-organized food service department operates. In almost all institutions, a full-time staff member who is experienced in food service management supervises food service operations. This individual is given the resources, authority, and responsibility to manage the department effectively, both in terms of labor and financial resources. The administrator of the food service department ordinarily supervises all the food service staff and others such as dieticians, bakers, and butchers. Depending on the system, a number of correctional officers may be assigned directly to the department also. More commonly, however, correctional staff are posted in the preparation and dining areas, but still work for the correctional department.

## Menu Preparation

Ordinarily, menus are prepared at least one week in advance. The administrator should plan all menus, including special diets, in connection with an independent review by a registered dietician. That review will ensure compliance with applicable nutritional standards, and it must be documented. Many institutions actually prepare longer menu cycles (the federal prison system, for instance, uses a 35-day cycle to reduce the monotony of short-cycle menu use.)

Menus should reflect the inmate population's cultural and ethnic preferences, as well as provide for their religious and medical needs. The menu for the current and next meals should be posted prominently near the entrance of the dining room, or near the start of the line. This convenient posting allows inmates to decide what items they want in advance, speeding the progress through the line. Ration items should be identified by quantity on the menu, as well as any special items that have medical or religious

implications, such as those with high sodium or pork content.

## Food Supplies and Storage

Food should be the best quality possible within the institution's budget, and of sufficient quantity to guarantee a wholesome diet. Available sources of food supplies depend largely on the nature and location of the institution. Common sources are local wholesale food distribution outlets, and contracts obtained through bidding to supply the institution for designated, quarterly periods. In rural institutions, an institutional farm may provide such items as fresh vegetables, meat, eggs, milk, butter, and cheese. Other items, such as cakes, pies, and bread, can be prepared in an inmate bakery. All foodstuffs should meet, or exceed, government inspection levels.

The delivery and storage system should ensure that food supplies are fresh, and delivered in a suitable condition. All incoming food not immediately used or processed in some way should be properly stored to prevent spoilage or waste. In most locations, a cold storage facility is available for such perishables as meat, milk, eggs, and fresh vegetables and fruits. Dried foods such as fruit, potatoes, and moist-dry foods may be stored in temperature-controlled storage rooms. Less perishable items like sugar, spices, crackers, and canned foods are best handled by a general storage facility. Shelf goods should be stored at temperatures of 45 to 80 degrees Fahrenheit; refrigerated foods maintained at 35 to 40 degrees Fahrenheit; and frozen foods kept at zero degrees Fahrenheit or below. Each refrigerated container or locker should have a thermometer on the door or exterior wall, so that staff can check these temperatures easily.

## Food Preparation

Food is usually prepared according to a standard recipe system that is available to all food service staff and inmate workers. This standard system ensures that the quantity and quality of meals are uniform from meal to meal, and that staff variables do not enter into the preparation. For this purpose, many institutions use the standard U.S. Navy system or the *Bureau of Prisons Food Service Manual* as their guides for food preparation.

Sanitation measures in the kitchen are absolutely critical. Each institution must have a daily cleaning and inspection system that ensures that the food preparation, storage, serving, and dining areas are totally clean. This is far more than a cosmetic issue. The health of every inmate and staff member in the institution hinges on the cleanliness of the food service area.

The personal habits and cleanliness of all food service staff and inmate workers are a constant concern. Adequate facilities for washing hands should be provided in the kitchen area. Clean white uniforms and aprons should always be available, and food handlers should be required to wear white hats while cooking or serving food; hair nets and serving gloves should be worn when appropriate.

## Special Diets

Special medical diets are made available to inmates, but only on medical authorization. Diet orders should be specific and complete, furnished in writing to the food service administrator, and rewritten monthly. Special diets should be kept as simple as possible, and should conform as closely as possible to the foods served other inmates.

A separate area in the kitchen under staff control may be used to store all diet trays, or they may be kept in a single hot cart behind the line for issue under staff direction. Many institutions use a diet card or pass system to ensure that only authorized inmates receive these meals.

Inmates also may have specific religious beliefs that require them to eat or not eat certain foods. Religious diets are ordinarily approved only by a chaplain. They should be specific and complete, furnished in writing to the food service manager; in many systems they, too, are reviewed periodically. An example would be Islamic inmates who are forbidden by their religion from contact with pork or pork products.

In the event a staff member observes an inmate approved for a special diet of any type eating

---

## ACA Food Service Standards

ACA standards for food service operations require that:

• The food service manager regularly inspect all areas and equipment related to food preparation, such as ranges, ovens, refrigerators, mixers, dishwashers, and garbage disposals, to ensure sanitary operating conditions; this equipment should be designed and located to allow efficient and thorough cleaning.

• Food handlers, at a minimum, must be in good health and free from communicable diseases and open or infected wounds.

• All people involved in preparing food are to be medically examined before, and periodically after, they begin working, in accord with local requirements for restaurants; this is to prevent individuals from transmitting illnesses, such as diarrhea or skin infections, to others via food or utensils.

---

unapproved foods, that fact should be reported to a supervisor so that the special diet status of that inmate can be reviewed.

## Meal Service

Gathering large numbers of inmates together presents a security risk under any circumstances. That fact makes the dining room a potential location for serious disturbances and incidents. As a result, it is critical that correctional staff enforce an orderly system of food lines and seating, as well as portion and utensil control.

The degree of staff supervision required and the nature of the institution's design will determine the system used for serving meals. To the extent possible, dining rooms should be designed to enhance the attractiveness of the meal-time atmosphere. Meals assume a magnified importance in inmates' daily routine, and are important to institutional personnel also. Thus, the condition and cleanliness of the kitchen and dining areas can influence an institution's entire atmosphere.

Food should be served as soon as possible after preparation, and at an appropriate temperature. Temperatures are ordinarily maintained by keeping the food items in warmers of some type, either cabinet- or pan-style. Direct service is usually from a steam table or some other type of cafeteria-style warming equipment.

Food distribution should be supervised at all times. Frequently, an inmate serving food will take advantage of an officer's temporary absence to "take care of" friends, or to not give other inmates their entitled portions.

The eating utensils used in a given institution should be based on a control system dictated by the type of population confined there. Many institutions use a full array of metal items, while others, particularly those with high-security populations, have gone to highly durable, washable plastic utensils. Control of eating utensils can be maintained by requiring inmates to dispose of them in a carefully positioned and supervised receptacle when they drop off their trays.

## Dining Room Routines

Inmates should be given enough time to wash before eating. Inmates working as painters or in other active occupations should be allowed to change clothing before entering the dining room.

Inmates must be fully clothed while in the dining room, and smoking should not be permitted at any time. Staff supervising the entrances should enforce the dress and smoking codes before inmates enter the

*Food service operations have an enormous effect on inmate morale and health.*

area. Staff can then also perform random inmate searches for weapons.

The dining room should provide normal group eating areas and permit conversation during dining hours. When possible, there should be "open" dining hours, thus reducing traditional waiting lines. Many facilities have eliminated forced seating based on housing unit, shop assignment, etc.

Serving and dining schedules should offer a reasonable amount of time for inmates to eat. When setting schedules, institutions with this kind of meal program must consider the types of food served, and the eating pattern of the inmates for that particular meal. Schedules are often set up according to housing units, but noon meals may be scheduled by work details.

Tables and chairs in the dining room should be arranged for good traffic flow and supervision; the actual arrangement will depend on the space available and the location of entrances and exits. Continuous rows of tables with adjacent aisles usually facilitate the orderly movement of inmates into the dining room, past the steam tables, and back to the eating tables.

The steam tables normally should be located next to the kitchen. This cafeteria-style arrangement usually permits enough supervisory space for officers to observe inmate activities on the line in all parts of the dining room. It also enables extra food to be passed out by inmate waiters after the first helping has been served to all inmates, in systems where that is done.

Even with the best of traffic flows, line cutting can be a problem. In the crowded dining room, there is great potential for a line-cutting dispute to develop into a far larger confrontation. Close staff supervision can deter this activity and prevent it from growing into a larger problem when it does occur.

Finally, the inmate dining room is not to be used as a shortcut to other areas, nor should inmates not assigned there be permitted to remain unless authorized. The dining room should not be used for loitering or congregating.

## Unit Dining Rooms

In some institutions, the prepared food portions are brought in bulk to the housing units, and served from smaller steam or electrical heating equipment. In these units, the inmates may eat in a common area, or in their cells, depending on the security level and the type of space available.

Unit dining rooms have some advantage for high-security institutions, because they eliminate the large numbers of inmates brought together by centralized dining. There are drawbacks, however, to these decentralized operations. Among them are the problems of food transportation and cleanup of multiple dining and food service areas. In addition, it is far easier for inmates to retain foodstuffs in their cells in this situation.

## Locked-Unit Operations

Food service in locked units is usually provided to inmates in their cells. In some units, selected inmates are permitted to eat in common areas in small groups. In these units, portable steam tables, microwave reheating, or thermal containers can be used successfully, and there are good reasons for using each in particular settings.

Locked-unit food service operations differ from institution to institution. However, there are several common principles that apply in almost all cases:

• All food carts should be thoroughly searched by staff for contraband being sent into the unit from cooperating inmates in the main kitchen area.

• No inmates should ever be used to serve food to other inmates in segregation status; this is a prime opportunity for pressure activity, as well as tampering with unpopular inmates' food.

• Inmates must be required to give back all utensils and other items on the food tray; this not only is for the safety of staff, but also because keeping food in cells is likely to attract vermin and insects.

• Staff should ensure that all inmates' meals arrive at their cells at the proper temperature.

• Food service supervisory personnel should regularly tour the locked units during mealtime, to ensure that they are properly served, with meals at the proper temperature.

## Commissary Operations

Home-cooked foods are seldom allowed in an institution. However, the commissary or inmate store is available in most locations for inmates to purchase a wider variety of discretionary food and other items. Selecting the articles to be sold in a commissary requires careful study. Most commissaries limit the selection to snacks and light foods that are not in conflict with the regular food program. Some items are virtually required, such as milk and sugar for coffee, in order to prevent kitchen theft from developing.

Moreover, if foods that need preparation are sold, then provisions for cooking, such as hot plates, "drops," and percolators, must be permitted, as well as proper utensils and a place to wash all of these items. Often this is impractical, particularly because refrigeration and proper sinks are not usually available in housing areas.

## Supervision Issues

Correctional officers are called on to provide area supervision in the food preparation and dining areas. These duties differ from institution to institution, but there are a number of common concerns that should be mentioned.

### Controlling Food Service Traffic

Traffic control in and out of the food service area is important. The unrestricted movement of inmates not only presents an accountability problem, but it also permits easier theft of food items, and pilferage of other contraband from the kitchen; the more traffic there is, the harder it will be to detect these items. For that reason, the kitchen area should be out of bounds

for all non-kitchen workers, and correctional staff should enforce that rule very closely.

### Searching Inmates

Searching inmates moving in and out of the institution is a companion issue. In addition to searches of inmates going into the area (to prevent the movement of weapons), searches of departing inmates are important. These deter food theft and reduce the likelihood that inmates will attempt to steal a kitchen knife or other hazardous contraband for use on the compound.

### Controlling Kitchen Items

Control of items coming into the kitchen through the loading dock is always a concern. The possibility of contraband coming in through regular food shipments from fixed sources of supply is quite high. Therefore, each institution should have a specific system for searching vehicles, loads, and drivers moving supplies into the compound. However, just because a delivery has been searched at the gate or in the receiving area does not mean that an officer assigned to the kitchen does not have to be concerned about this issue. The contraband could have been overlooked, or placed in the supplies after they arrived and were searched. In any event, officers should never assume that any items in warehouses, storage areas, or even in the preparation areas are totally contraband-free.

### Controlling Trash

Trash control is a related issue, particularly relevant to escape attempts. Every facility has a different process for collecting, securing, and removing trash from the compound. The general rule, however, is that any trash truck or dumpster load should be kept locked in a sallyport-type area through one or more counts, to be sure that no inmates are

*Correctional officers must ensure that proper security and supervision practices are observed in the food preparation area, that distribution of food is fair, and that order is maintained in the dining area.*

hidden inside. Probing and other search techniques may be used also. The same concerns and search techniques should be used for boxes or containers of food prepared inside and sent to satellite camps or other locations; inmates can be hidden in those containers also.

Trash compactors, too, are an avenue for escape. Inmates have successfully (and at times unsuccessfully) fabricated skeletal frameworks or "crushproof" containers to hide in to escape from a dumpster. Sallyporting is the safest way to eliminate this as a likely avenue for escape attempts.

## Controlling Kitchen Tools

Tool control in the kitchen consists primarily of knife control. However, in facilities with butcher shops, saws and other tools used in those processes can be dangerous as well. In most facilities, kitchen tools are stored in a locked cabinet in a secure area. Inside the cabinet, the tools are hung on hooks, behind which are painted the shadow of the tool, so it is easy to see if any are missing. When an inmate or staff member checks out the tool, a durable metal tag with that person's name or other identifier is placed on the hook, so that it is clear who has that item. A written inventory list of all items in the cabinet should be kept in it, and at each shift the responsible staff member should check the inventory and initial the list. This inventory should also be jointly checked with a correctional staff member on a regular basis, not less than monthly.

## Yeast and Extract Control

Yeast and extract control is another concern in an institution. Yeast can be used to make home-brew alcoholic beverages, and many extracts have alcohol in them. These items should be kept under lock and key,

with a strict inventory maintained. Even yeast residues (the wrappers or containers, for instance) should be disposed of by staff outside the institution, because the small amount of remaining yeast is enough to start fermentation.

In this connection, inmates with large amounts of sugar or fruits, or even small amounts of unbaked bread in their possession, should be viewed with suspicion as potential brew makers. Even if the institution does not have a possession limit on these food items, an officer encountering them in large amounts should refer the matter to a supervisor for advice.

Inmates have a tremendous amount of ingenuity when it comes to finding places to brew alcoholic drinks. While it is impossible to list all the likely places, staff should know that tubes, pipes, and elaborate equipment are not necessary—brew has been made in every possible simple container, from toilets to garbage bags. Locations include cells, job sites, behind ovens, in pipe chases, and anywhere that temperatures are likely to stay warm and staff are not likely to suspect. In short, ingenuity is the only limit to where brew can be made.

## Accommodating Inmate Work Assignments

Using food as payment for work, or as a special privilege, is unjustified and should never be permitted. When inmates work in outlying jobs, or on odd shifts, it often is necessary to provide lunches or extra food to cover the shift portion of the day. Some institutions take into account the fact that some work assignments are more physically demanding than others, and provide extra rations from leftovers. Often, larger lunches are needed for farm workers who work extra hours during harvesting and for night workers in a dairy or piggery. In cases like this, supervisory staff, not line employees, should decide who gets what, and how much.

## Summary

Nutritious and tasteful meals, served in a pleasant and safe environment, have great significance in an institution. This is true not only because food takes on magnified importance in the institutional setting, but also because the dining area can be a breeding ground for serious disturbances.

Although food service responsibilities are typically assigned to a food service manager, the correctional officer must ensure that proper security and supervision practices are observed in the food preparation area, that distribution of food is fair, and that order is maintained in the dining area.

*APPLICABLE ACA STANDARDS*

Food Services: 3-4294 to 3-4309

# 9

# Sanitation and Hygiene

Overcrowding in correctional institutions is of increasing concern today. Outdated or poorly designed correctional institutions are the realities that many correctional administrators live with—institutions that are hard to maintain and keep in a high state of sanitation. And yet the demands of congregate living mean that it is even more important now than ever before to emphasize sanitation in institutions, and the important hygienic steps needed to ensure inmate health.

An effective sanitation program raises inmate and staff morale; no one likes to live or work in a dirty, smelly, poorly maintained institution. Ironically, some of the least expensive and most effective improvements in the atmosphere of an institution can be made with soap and water, disinfectant, and inmate labor. The only essentials are the necessary administrative support and supervisory initiative.

## The Role of Supervisors

Sanitation is an area where supervisory standards are critical. If the warden and other top staff do not personally set high standards of hygiene and sanitation, and if they are not active in setting up programs to enact those high standards, then a clean, sanitary institution will not be achieved.

Individual correctional officers, on their own initiative, can have a tremendous positive impact in this area, but for an entire institution to be neat, clean, and orderly, the administration must set and maintain high standards and expectations.

Once those standards are communicated to mid-level and line staff, then other systems must be in place to support those efforts. Those systems include regular purchase of the proper equipment and supplies, systematic inspections of the institution, and prompt corrective action when deficiencies are found. Maintenance staff involvement is an important part of this effort.

## The Inspection System

The institution must be inspected at least annually by appropriate officials to ensure the health of personnel and inmates. In addition, all institutional areas should be inspected at least weekly by a designated staff member (often the safety or sanitation officer), who should submit a written report to the appropriate department for corrective action, and any supervisory copies as required by local policy.

The sanitation and safety system also should include regular inspections by unit and area staff. Moreover, supervisory correctional staff should inspect the institution as part of their daily routine. This is not only necessary for sanitation itself, but for the supervisors to have the opportunity to keep in touch with the actual job performance of the line employees.

Individual room or dormitory inspections are a regular part of most institutional routines, and inmates whose living areas are not acceptably clean should be recalled from wherever they are and required to complete the job. In extreme cases, disciplinary action may be needed to bring a specific inmate's room into compliance.

Unit inspections should also include non-cell areas like showers, toilets, and sinks, as well as ventilators, fan outlets, light fixtures, and other parts of the unit that are not often cleaned in the day-to-day course of business. These sanitation inspections should not be confused with security inspections, which are

*Some of the least expensive and most effective improvements in the atmosphere of an institution can be made with soap and water, disinfectant, and inmate labor.*

intended to detect deficiencies in the security hardware and construction of the institution.

## Living Quarters

Each institution, and every housing unit in it, should have a clearly defined program for daily cleaning. This program should include the use of inmate orderlies for cleaning common areas, as well as individual inmates' responsibility for their own living areas.

### Standards for Unit and Cell Upkeep

The standards for unit and cell upkeep should specify that dirt and trash are not allowed to accumulate in any part of a living area; when a consistent, high standard of cleanliness is maintained, there is less need for dramatic cleanup activity. Pre-identified areas are ordinarily assigned to specific inmate orderlies, and unit officers should inspect their work when it is done. These duties should include specified tasks like mopping floors, and waxing when appropriate. Standards for waxing floors and

maintaining unit common areas such as dayrooms and showers should be a clear part of the institution's overall sanitation plan. A supply system should be in place that permits staff and inmates access to necessary cleaning materials.

### Personal Property Policy

Personal property policy should clearly state the quantities of food purchased in the institution store or commissary that are permitted in cells. Foods that attract vermin should not be allowed in cells, except as otherwise provided.

In overcrowded institutions, a large amount of personal property can make an already small housing area seem smaller. For that reason, controlling personal property is an important part of maintaining not only a sanitary institution, but one that is neat and uncluttered. Clear limits on the amount and type of personal property in cells or dormitories will prevent them from becoming cluttered fire hazards. Insisting on reasonable amounts of personal property also aids security, because it is far simpler for officers to search more modest amounts of property.

Inmates should not be permitted to hang sheets, blankets, or any other items on bars and windows, which might obscure visibility into a living area. These visual barriers prevent staff from properly supervising the interior of cells and dormitories, allowing inmates to engage in improper behavior. Hanging items also constitute a fire hazard. For many of the same reasons, many institutions limit the number of pictures or other materials that can be placed on cell walls.

Wires, antennas, cables, and hanging plants also should be regulated in housing areas. Not only do they constitute a general safety hazard, but they are unsightly and contribute to the unit's overall cluttered, crowded appearance.

### Toilet Facilities

Toilet facilities must be maintained at a high level of cleanliness. These are areas where disease transmission potential is quite high, and staff must take every necessary step to be sure that all toilets and urinals are regularly cleaned and disinfected.

Likewise, sinks in cells and congregate areas must be maintained at a very high level. Not only is it personally offensive to anyone to have to wash in a dirty sink, perhaps caked with the soap scum residue and hairs of a dozen others, but it is clearly creating a high risk for disease transmission. Officers in housing areas must place a high degree of emphasis on this area.

### Bathing Facilities

There should be sufficient bathing facilities in housing areas to permit general-population inmates to shower at least three times a week. In institutions where there is cellblock bathing, bathing facilities must be maintained in a sanitary condition at all times, with regular scrubbing of all surfaces to avoid soap film and moldy buildup. In many institutions, a regular schedule of bathing is used, and in those locations, inmates should proceed directly to the shower at the designated time and, after bathing is completed, return to their cells.

For institutions with a central bathing/clothing issue system, at the conclusion of the bathing period, the officer should supervise the clothing count, check the laundry slips, and sign and place them inside the laundry bags with the soiled clothing. A duplicate record should be kept in the cellblock office to ensure proper counts and amounts of clothing are being returned. Upon return, clean clothing should be checked carefully and stored in the clothing room for distribution.

## Upkeep of Non-Unit Areas

The non-unit areas of the institution should be subject to a structured cleaning system as well. Some areas require cleaning only once a week; others once a day or shift; still others need constant cleaning, like corridor areas near doorways in inclement weather. It is up to local staff to set up a schedule that meets the institution's needs, realizing that inmate labor is plentiful. Cleaning activities should be supervised at all times to ensure that work performed is proper and thorough. Particular attention should be paid to keeping the facility's floors clean, dry, and free of hazardous substances.

## Shop and Work Areas

Shop sanitation is important for several reasons. First, a cluttered and disorganized shop is an unsafe shop. Second, unclean working conditions in a kitchen or warehouse can breed disease or vermin just as easily as in a housing unit. Finally, the

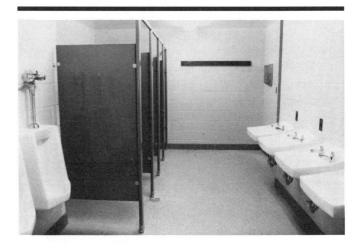

*For an entire institution to be neat, clean, and orderly, the administration must set and maintain high standards and expectations.*

housekeeping conditions in a work area telegraph something about the general security and supervision provided in that area. Supervisors who permit dirty, cluttered work areas are also likely to permit lax tool or key control, and are probably not as concerned about inmate supervision.

## Yards and Other Outdoor Areas

The institution's overall housekeeping plan should also provide for regular cleaning of all outdoor areas, including the yard, interior courtyards, and interior building facades. This should include a well-defined system of inmate orderlies or groundskeepers, with specific areas of responsibility. In general, these inmates should be supervised by staff on the ground, but some additional coverage can be provided by tower officers in secure locations. In particular, tower officers should be concerned about watching for unusual activity on the part of these yard workers, who might indicate they were assisting or participating in any escape or contraband-related activity.

## Cleaning Sensitive Areas

Higher security areas, or those with clear security implications, should never be cleaned by inmates.

This category ordinarily includes the control center, armory, key storage area or lock shop, and towers. Staff should have a regular system for cleaning these important areas.

## Preventive Maintenance Program

An institution without a well-structured preventive maintenance program is a facility that inevitably is going to deteriorate. First, the maintenance department should have a schedule for reviewing the institution's equipment and repair needs. Repetitive maintenance tasks, such as painting and filter changing, can be scheduled.

However, it also is vital that officers who observe conditions requiring maintenance and repair have a clearly defined system for reporting those conditions to the proper department as they occur. Once that is done, a properly designed system will include a method for supervisory follow-up to ensure that the required work is completed.

## Waste Disposal and Pest Control

Waste disposal and pest control programs are essential to maintaining a sanitary institution. These programs include regular inspections for pest and rodent infestation and proper documentation. Most institutions also have contracts with licensed pest control professionals, who are readily available to provide pest control services. Liquid and solid wastes must be collected, stored, and disposed of in a manner that protects the health and safety of inmates, staff, and visitors. To do this effectively, most institutions have a regular trash pickup and disposal system. Staff will determine the best methods for the particular institution for pickup, short-term storage inside, and outside movement of refuse. Any hazardous wastes generated in shops or industrial operations should be controlled in line with local policy and disposed of in line with state and federal regulations.

Since regular trash movement out of the institution is a prime escape route, each institution has a particular routine for ensuring that inmates do not hide in the trash truck, dumpster, or other receptacle for garbage, industrial waste, etc. Most of these include keeping the container or vehicle locked in a sallyport or other area through one or more good counts before allowing it to go outside the perimeter.

## Laundry Programs

All inmates should have clothing that fits properly, suits the climate, and meets their needs. All government clothing and bedding supplies issued to an inmate are that inmate's responsibility and the inmate is held responsible for their use and care.

It is critical to have facilities for thoroughly cleaning, disinfecting, and storing government-issued inmate clothing. Every effort must be made to maintain a high standard of inmate laundry services.

In some locations, inmates are permitted to have their own clothing, and in others, none is allowed. For that reason, the issue, storage, cleaning, and

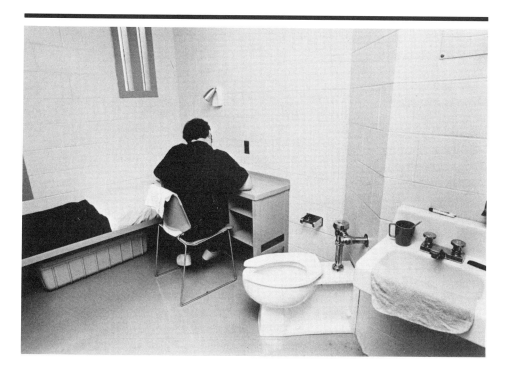

*The standards for unit and cell upkeep should specify that dirt and trash are not allowed to accumulate in any part of a living area.*

accountability systems in place will be entirely different in each institution. In general, though, if the institution permits personal clothing, then a system must be available that provides reasonable assurances against theft in the laundry process. The inmate's personal clothes must be returned with a minimum of delay, each inmate receiving his or her own clothes from the laundry. In many locations, however, this personal clothing system takes the form of laundry equipment in the housing units, with the inmates washing their own clothes. Where the institution does provide clothing, a central laundry is often used, with a centralized clothing exchange based on inmate register number, bin numbers, or some other system.

All inmates must be supplied with adequate bedding and linens. In most institutions this takes the form of standard issue items, but in a few facilities, personal linens are permitted, using the unit laundry system to keep them clean. Where linens are issued, a regular exchange program is used, and sheets and pillowcases are typically changed and laundered at least weekly; blankets should be laundered monthly and sterilized before reissue. Mattresses should be aired at regular intervals.

Protective and special clothing is ordinarily issued to inmates assigned to the institution's food service, hospital, farm, garage, plant maintenance shops, and other special work details. Special laundry procedures are ordinarily established for these items.

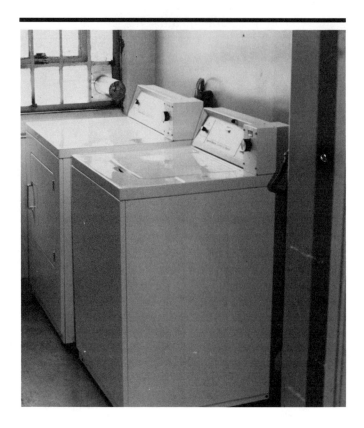

## Hair Care Services

Facilities are provided in most institutions where inmates can obtain needed hair care services. A central barber shop, a single room in the cellhouse, or any multipurpose room may be used. In any event, hair should be cut under sanitary conditions and in an area that permits observation by officers.

Equipment and supplies should be stored securely when not in use. Scissors, razors, and any other hazardous items should be controlled like any other Class A (highly dangerous) tool—shadowed, checked out, and inventoried at least daily.

Female institutions with more elaborate hair care facilities should carefully review the chemicals used in various hair treatments. Some contain highly caustic or poisonous materials, and should be used under controlled circumstances, if at all. Portable hair dryers or other items that have significant security implications should be controlled as Class A items.

## Summary

One of the major responsibilities of any institution is maintaining inmate health. Proper sanitation and hygiene are major ingredients in this process, and also improve the morale of those who live or work in an institution.

A decline in personal hygiene may signal a personal problem on the part of an inmate, and a drop in overall sanitation or hygiene in an institution can similarly indicate major supervisory problems at one or more levels.

While the actual housekeeping and maintenance chores may not be a direct responsibility of the correctional officer, the supervision of these activities is. In addition to being aware of proper procedures to follow for sanitation, the officer should immediately report any condition that may affect the health and safety of an inmate or staff member.

*APPLICABLE ACA STANDARDS*

Sanitation and Hygiene: 3-4134 and 3-4310 to 3-4325

# 10

## Health Care

When the state confines individuals, it deprives them of the opportunity to choose their own personal health care. In doing that, the state must then assume responsibility for providing at least basic health care for these individuals. It is the institution's responsibility to maintain physical and mental health care services, and to take necessary steps to prevent serious illnesses and accidents in the inmate population. For the purposes of this chapter, medical and dental care are covered together under the general term "medical."

Failure to adequately meet the duty to provide adequate health care can be cruel and unusual punishment, a constitutional violation. However, negligence (sometimes called medical malpractice) or a simple disagreement between an inmate and doctor over treatment do not constitute cruel and unusual punishment. (Of course, negligence and malpractice are unacceptable and may become the basis for successful legal action.)

ACA standards provide a picture of how a good institutional health care system should be set up. They require institutions to have a designated health authority who is responsible in a well-defined way for health care services. The health authority may be a physician, health administrator, private health contractor, or government health agency. Even when this authority is not a staff physician, final medical judgments still must be made by a designated physician from some other source.

It is important to remember that whether a particular inmate needs medical care is a matter to be decided by trained medical personnel. The officer on duty in the cellhouse, the shop supervisor, or other nonmedical employees should not unnecessarily restrict or control inmate access to medical personnel who can decide when medical care is needed.

The institution also must have available to inmates the services of an adequately equipped medical facility that meets the legal requirements for a licensed general hospital with respect to the services it offers. If the institution does not have its own licensed hospital inside (and many do not), it will ordinarily have an infirmary for basic care inside the institution, and provide hospital care through a contract with an outside hospital.

In every facility, space should be provided where inmates can be examined and treated in private. In an institution's health services area, the type of space available and equipment in the examination or treatment room depend on whether it is an infirmary or a full-scale hospital, as well as on the qualifications of the medical staff. Equipment should be checked and tested periodically by properly qualified medical or technical staff, but security personnel should be satisfied that it is properly secured from inmate access.

## Initial Medical Contacts

In addition to any initial medical intake screening, all inmates should receive a full medical screening upon their arrival at the facility, as part of the admission procedures. These screenings, using a combination of specific questions about the inmates' medical history, tests, and observation, are designed to prevent newly arrived inmates who pose a health or safety threat to themselves or others from being admitted to the facility's general population. Test results, particularly for communicable diseases, should be received and evaluated before an inmate is assigned to housing in the general population, or assigned a job. Initial screenings ordinarily are performed by health care personnel; in some institutions they are done by a health-care trained correctional officer at the time of admission.

## Sick Call

Since it is not practical for an institution to allow inmates to leave their jobs or housing units whenever they want to go to the infirmary or hospital, some form of routine sick call is used in almost all correctional institutions, except for emergencies. This ordinarily consists of an appointment sign-up procedure; it also can be a specific time when inmates can go to the hospital for screening and, if necessary, a full examination by a nurse, physician's assistant, or a physician. No member of the correctional staff should actually approve or disapprove inmate requests for attendance at sick call. Sick call is ordinarily initiated by the inmate, but officers should consider unusual respiratory conditions (such as a severe cough, complaints of pain in the chest, obvious indications of a severe cold, elevation of temperature, severe stomach complaints, abdominal cramps, nausea, or vomiting) as causes to send individuals to sick call.

After screening or examination at sick call by a doctor or other health care provider, further treatment may be needed. In many locations, this involves issuing a series of passes that allow the inmate to visit clinics. In some cases, it may involve transportation to an outside hospital or clinic.

When sick calls reach large proportions they can become disruptive to other institutional programs and routines. Some institutions hold sick call when most people are out on recreation, or actually have a medical staff person hold a sick call screening at the larger job sites, like the industries building. These strategies deter malingerers or other inmates who would otherwise use the sick call procedures for nonmedical purposes.

## Medication Issues

Inmates who are approved for medication cannot just walk down to the hospital when they feel like it to receive their medication. Instead, regular, prescribed medication is given out in most institutions in a "pill line" or some other organized form. Medications are dispensed by a medical staff member, who makes sure the inmates take the medicine then. In addition, staff note on the inmates' medication chart or other medical record the fact that the medication was taken.

In locked units, the medical staff ordinarily may dispense medication at the same time they hold sick call rounds. Inmates in these units should be watched carefully to be sure they have actually swallowed their

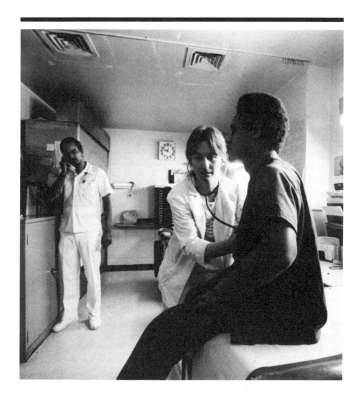

*Failure to adequately meet the duty to provide adequate health care can be cruel and unusual punishment, a constitutional violation.*

medication, particularly any inmates who may be thought to be potentially suicidal, or those who may be pressured into selling or giving away their medication.

### Drug Storage

Drug storage is a different issue. Any large institution, even one that has only an infirmary, will have a great many controlled medications in stock for its population. No inmates should *ever* be permitted in a drug storage area or be given access to any bulk supplies of drugs.

Drugs for daily use should be kept in separate, carefully inventoried containers that can be accounted for from shift to shift. When not dispensing medication from these containers (usually storage cabinets of some type), staff must secure them at all times and keep them in a secure area.

Some institutions have an emergency bag or rolling "crash" cart that can be moved by staff to the

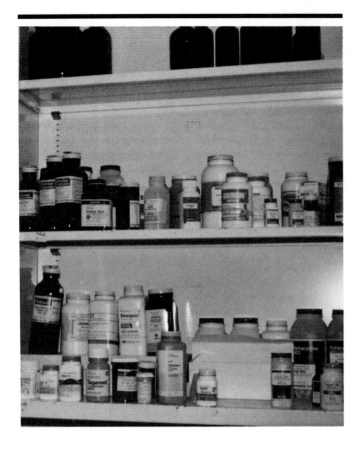

be used. There are, however, some common concerns in all such trips.

Escorting staff should search the inmate and clothing to be worn on the trip when they take custody. Assuming someone else has searched the inmates, or searched them as thoroughly as necessary, has been a problem in many instances where inmates later produced handcuff keys or weapons.

Weapons should never be allowed to come in contact with an inmate under escort. While there is considerable variation on this theme in different agencies, the risks of armed escort staff coming in contact with inmates is an extreme concern. Local procedures should take this into account, as well as the need to regulate inmate contact with visitors and the public, and the issue of when to remove restraints on patients undergoing treatment.

## Supervision Issues in the Hospital or Infirmary

Supervising inmate traffic in and out of the hospital is an important task for correctional staff assigned to the medical area. There ordinarily is a pass or door check system of some type in place that will be used to account for all inmates coming to the medical area. Officers should be aware of the need for close supervision of every inmate who comes into the area.

One of the reasons for this is the fact that in addition to drugs, needles and syringes are kept in the hospital. Unless proper controls are maintained over these hazardous items, they can easily fall into inmate hands and be used to inject drugs, not to mention the risk of AIDS being transmitted through used needles. Most institutions have a needle and syringe accountability and storage program similar to that for controlled medications. To that should be added the need to maintain secure, safe custody of used needles and syringes, and to properly and safely dispose of them in line with applicable state and local health regulations. At most locations, they are stored in a locked container until crushed and burned outside the compound.

## Common Emergencies

The use of emergency passes to the infirmary or hospital is ordinarily kept to a minimum. When an inmate's problem is clearly not an emergency, the inmate should be urged to wait for the next regular sick call. However, if the inmate becomes upset, refuses to work, or insists on seeing a doctor, it is wiser to agree. In addition, each institution has specific procedures to follow if the problem is clearly an emergency requiring immediate care.

scene of a medical crisis. These containers, or any other emergency drug supply, should be kept in a locked area as well, with an inventory posted in it, which is also checked from shift to shift.

Bulk storage of medications should be in a vault or large safe, to which the combination is closely restricted. Each agency has a different process for entering this vault, replenishing daily or weekly supplies, and inventorying its contents. However, at least once a month, the vault should be inventoried jointly by a responsible medical supervisor and supervisory correctional staff.

Newly purchased medications should not be delivered to the inside warehouse or storeroom, where they might be pilfered by inmates. Instead, a responsible medical staff person should pick them up outside the secure compound, and move them to the bulk storage area, ideally when there are no inmates on the compound. They should, of course, be added to the inventory as soon as they are brought to the vault.

## Medical Trips

In some cases, inmates must be transported outside the institution for medical or dental treatment. Each agency has different procedures for the use of restraints, number of escorts, and types of weapons to

# No inmates should ever be permitted in a drug storage area or be given access to any bulk supplies of drugs.

First aid kits are often available in designated areas of the facility. The medical staff should approve the contents, number, location, and procedures for monthly inspection of the kits. Contents of first aid kits typically include roller gauze, sponges, triangle bandages, adhesive tape, adhesive bandages, etc. They do not include emergency drugs. The contents should be inventoried regularly and replenished after each use.

Most institutions provide some type of emergency first aid training to staff. The officer must clearly evaluate each emergency on its own, but after calling for assistance, some situations may require the officer to provide emergency care. First aid training should include familiarity with the following reactions to inmate emergencies: serious bleeding, unconsciousness, heart attack, shock, convulsions, choking, heat exhaustion, nosebleed, eye irritations, poisoning, burns, and broken bones. Although officers should be prepared to react to these emergencies, medical personnel should be notified at once in any medical situation.

## Cardiopulmonary Resuscitation (CPR)

In a heart attack, the victim's heart stops functioning normally, and the blood flow to it and the other parts of the body stops. If this stoppage continues for more than a minute or two, brain damage will occur. CPR has proved effective many times in keeping oxygen flowing to the brain of heart attack victims long enough for the heart to either spontaneously recover part of its function, or for other assistance to arrive.

CPR is a technique for assisting a failing heart to pump blood to the brain through direct chest pressure, and to get oxygen into the blood by helping the victim's breathing. Many institutions teach CPR to all staff in the regular training program. It is not

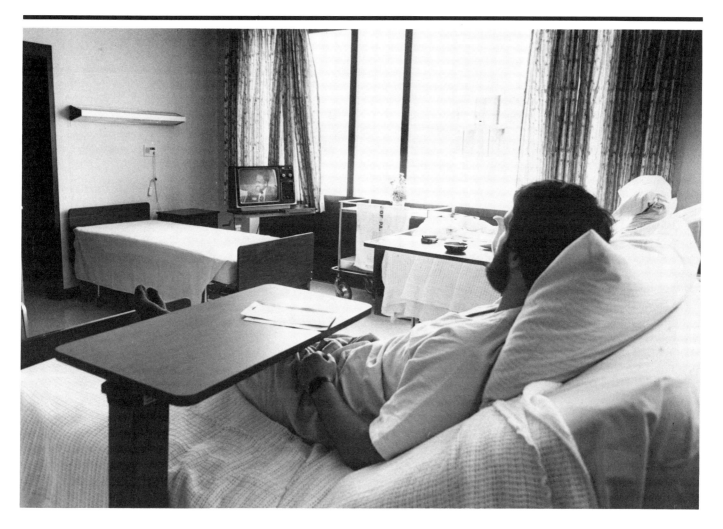

possible to teach CPR in a publication—it must be learned with actual practice of the techniques involved.

## Medical Services in Locked Units

Inmates in locked units cannot go to sick call or pill line. Medical services must be brought to them. Typically, medical staff such as physicians' assistants travel to the unit once each shift, and make rounds of the cells, screening any inmates who have complaints. If necessary, they can be moved (under escort, in restraints, when appropriate) to the medical area for further examination or treatment. Likewise, medications are dispensed to inmates in their cells, ordinarily by medical staff when they make their rounds.

## Acquired Immune Deficiency Syndrome (AIDS)

AIDS is an as-yet incurable, fatal disease caused by a virus known as the Human Immunodeficiency Virus (HIV). When the HIV enters a person's bloodstream, it attacks certain types of white blood cells (the cells that fight all kinds of diseases), weakening and eventually destroying the body's immune system (the ability to fight disease). As a result of the extensively damaged immune system that develops over time, the individual becomes unable to fight off other infections or cancers and dies.

Since the discovery of the virus that causes AIDS and the development of blood tests to detect HIV infection, there has been confusion about the term "AIDS." When a person first becomes infected with the HIV virus, there are usually no significant symptoms. In fact, symptoms may not develop until the individual's immune system has become badly damaged.

As the body's immune system becomes increasingly weakened by the HIV infection, the individual develops certain symptoms or signs. This stage is commonly referred to as AIDS Related Complex (ARC), although there is no clearly defined medical diagnosis of ARC the way there is for AIDS. This ARC condition confirms that the person is infected with the HIV virus, but the infection has not progressed to the actual AIDS.

### AIDS Diagnosis

The diagnosis of AIDS is not actually made until a secondary opportunistic infection occurs—an infection that takes advantage of the opportunity to attack the person's weakened immune system. This is usually not until several years after the initial infection, but because experience with the disease has been relatively short, this may not always be the case. A person could be infected with the HIV virus (the AIDS virus) for years, and even have some symptoms due to that infection, but would not be considered to actually have AIDS until the first opportunistic infection (or cancer) occurs. This definition is under constant study and continues to undergo gradual changes.

Individuals with certain combinations of positive HIV tests are presumed to be infected with the HIV virus, even though they may show no symptoms and appear healthy. As is true of any test, there is always a *small* possibility that the test result is an error. Individuals who test positive for the HIV virus, yet have had no opportunistic infection, are frequently referred to as "having been exposed to the HIV virus." This terminology is misleading, however, since it does not make clear that such individuals are almost certainly infected with that virus.

### How the HIV Virus Is Transmitted

Cases of HIV infection occur primarily in homosexual and bisexual men, in intravenous drug users of both sexes, and in sexual partners of individuals in these groups. There is no evidence that the HIV virus is spread through casual contact with

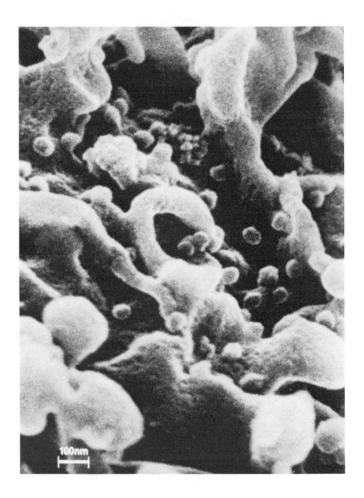

100nm

# The wisest course of action for an individual officer is to assume that the bodily fluids of every inmate are contaminated with the HIV virus.

an infected person, such as contact in family settings, prisons, schools, or anywhere people live or work together.

While HIV can be found in other bodily fluids, it is almost always found in blood and sexual fluids. It is clear the virus must be transmitted into the bloodstream of an individual, even if the source is sexual fluid.

The virus is not easily transmitted from one person to another except when certain dangerous practices are involved. All evidence indicates the virus is transmitted primarily through two routes:

• *Blood to blood contact*—usually by shared needles through intravenous drug use
• *Sexual fluids to blood contact*—occurs in certain sexual practices, particularly by male homosexuals engaging in anal intercourse; transmission through vaginal intercourse also has been documented

Transmission of HIV occurs much less frequently by heterosexual contact than between homosexuals. Transmission of the virus during pregnancy, from a mother to her fetus, may frequently occur. In addition, the virus may be transmitted through the transfusion of blood during surgery or other medical procedures, for instance, during transfusion of blood products in the treatment of hemophilia or other diseases. However, blood and blood products are now screened for the HIV virus in all blood banking procedures.

The HIV virus is *not* transmitted:

• Through casual contact with infected individuals
• Through the air
• Through contact with nonliving objects
• Through mosquito bites or other insect contacts
• Among health care personnel and patients, except in rare instances, even after repeated or extreme exposure (through contaminated needle puncture or the mishandling of infected material/laboratory specimens)
• Deep kissing, bites or by external contact with blood or sexual fluids (if these fluids do not enter open wounds)

AIDS is a fatal disease, and for now, no clearly established treatment exists for those infected with the HIV virus. However, depending on the cause and type of the opportunistic, or secondary infection, many patients may be successfully treated on an illness-by-illness basis. In addition, there are medications and treatments under study that may prove at least partially successful in treating the basic HIV infection. The development of an AIDS vaccine is also being researched, but is possibly years away.

## Prevention of Infection

At present, it appears that those most at risk for AIDS are people who engage in high-risk practices, such as drug-needle use and certain homosexual practices. To the extent that those high-risk behaviors can be prevented, transmission of AIDS can be reasonably controlled. For staff, the issue usually is not sharing needles or sex with inmates, but with preventing excessive exposure to bodily fluids through an accident or other incident, even though such exposures are unlikely to result in transmission of the HIV virus.

The most important weapon to prevent HIV infection in prison is education of both staff and inmates, not just those in high-risk categories. Emphasis must be placed on the cause and transmission of this disease, with special emphasis on safe sexual practices and the avoidance of indiscriminate sexual contacts, multiple partners, and contaminated needles and other paraphernalia common among intravenous drug users. Similarly, emphasis must be placed on the ways the disease is not transmitted, in order to reassure those who are poorly informed. In an institution, sexual activity and drug use are contrary to regulations anyway, so normal supervision and security practices can also deter and reduce the transmission of this disease. The approach to individuals concerned about possible HIV infection must be reassuring and responsive. In most systems, inmates requesting an HIV test are given one, and that can be the starting point for counseling and education about high-risk behavior.

## Institutional Handling of AIDS Cases

Testing procedures for incoming inmates may include a blood test for AIDS, but that is not true in all locations. As a result, staff members may not know if any particular inmate is HIV-positive, meaning that he or she might be capable of transmitting AIDS. In addition, most states and the federal government have strict rules on confidentiality of medical records, which means that even if the medical staff knew an inmate was HIV-positive, they might not be able to tell other staff.

The probability that correctional officers or other staff will contract HIV infection from inmates is so small as to be virtually nonexistent, even under extreme circumstances. However, the wisest course of action for an individual officer is to assume that the

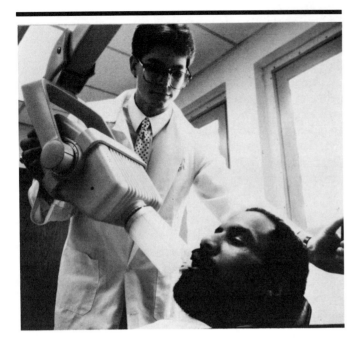

work closely with medical personnel, other staff, and patients in proper health management and education.

## Epilepsy

The human brain operates with very mild electrical activity. Epilepsy results (for various reasons) from disturbances in these electrical patterns or rhythms in the brain. Many epileptic seizures can be provoked by periods of emotional excitement. Thus, if epileptics get upset, they may have a "spell."

Epilepsy may result in any one or all of these symptoms: seizures, which are often called "fits" or "spells" (convulsions); impairment of motor control (falling); loss of consciousness; and psychological difficulties. There are three main seizure types: the "grand mal," "petit mal," and "psychomotor episodes."

During "grand mal" seizures, people lose consciousness and have violent convulsions. They black out at first, become stiff, and barely breathe; this is followed by severe muscle twitching and shaking of the body. Breathing can be so restricted that the person turns blue. There can also be frothing at the mouth. Sometimes, the bowels or the bladder are emptied during the course of an attack. Many epileptics experience a warning feeling (called an aura), so they can to some extent protect themselves before the attack by lying down; but most do not and are taken suddenly by a seizure. Some epileptics involuntarily emit a cry before their attack begins. Such spells are usually followed by a period of confusion and lethargy.

In the "petit mal" epileptic seizure the person is not aware of what is going on around him or her. Even though there is no actual convulsion, these epileptics might be hurt by their inability to respond to emergencies or even routine tasks, and may be injured by moving machinery. These episodes rarely last more than 30 seconds, after which the individual returns to normal.

During the "psychomotor" epileptic seizure, individuals do not experience a convulsion, but do experience reduced consciousness and loss of memory. They retain the ability to act, but usually in a purposeless fashion, often talking nonsense, making chewing movements with their mouth or displaying other bizarre behavior.

### Response to a Seizure

The emergency treatment of an epileptic convulsion first involves the understanding that it must run its course; there is nothing one can do to stop it. During a major attack, the person will very likely thrash about violently. A pillow or substitute, such as a coat, may be placed under the person's head to prevent damage to the skull. Nearby objects,

bodily fluids of every inmate are contaminated. That way, the chance of even accidentally picking up the virus through an inmate contact is reduced. This does not mean that a staff member should not provide normal services or have normal contacts with inmates. It does mean, however, that when there are incidents like stabbings or other emergencies, where blood or other body fluids may be exposed, the employee should carefully follow agency policy and practices in minimizing the risks involved.

While some correctional systems have decided to separate all HIV-positive cases in one location, most have not. In most institutions, inmates with the HIV virus are not isolated, segregated, or otherwise specially managed, except when their medical condition warrants it. However, inmates who are HIV-positive, and who are sexually active in prison or who are predatory and may assault others, are ordinarily placed in long-term detention status to protect staff and others.

The attitude of staff toward individuals with AIDS should be as supportive, understanding, reassuring, and responsive as possible. These people have a fatal disease. Some systems set up special counseling programs or other individualized treatment for them, and to the extent the law allows, some are released as they near death, so they can be in a more normal setting for the final weeks or months of their life.

Because it is not practical to discuss in this guidebook the many AIDS-related situations that may occur in various correctional systems and in different judicial districts throughout the country, correctional staff should seek guidance from supervisors. Regardless of these differences, staff should be aware of the specific policy for handling such cases at their institutions. To the degree that they can, they should on which the inmate could be injured, should be removed. If the person seems to be choking, he or she might have involuntarily forced his or her tongue into the back of the mouth, closing off the air intake. Roll the person over on the side, so that the tongue can be coughed out. Tight clothing, such as a belt or closely fitted collar, should be loosened. After the uncontrolled thrashing phase is over, let the person rest or sleep and recover. The other types of seizures will not ordinarily require this kind of active assistance.

### Treatment

The long-term medical treatment of epilepsy involves a physician prescribing specific medications. It is important to remember that when such drugs are prescribed, it is critical for the inmate to take them. Some epilepsy-controlling medications may represent a temptation to other inmates in the population. Also, some epileptics resist taking their medication because of the possible side effects, such as drowsiness. For these reasons, their dispensation should be closely supervised, ideally by a trained medical staff member. Also, when possible, use liquid forms of medicine.

## Diabetes

The human body requires certain chemicals, which it produces, to use foods that we eat. One of these chemicals is insulin, which helps the body use sugars properly.

A diabetic is a person whose body produces either too little, or an inactive supply of, insulin. Unless there is a proper balance of sugar and insulin, the body is unable to operate efficiently, and the person becomes ill. Thus, treatment or control is based on either controlling the amount of sugar the body has to deal with, adding insulin from an outside source, or stimulating the body's natural insulin production in some way.

Diet is a diabetic's fundamental key to controlling the condition. Almost half the known diabetics have enough natural insulin to maintain satisfactory control by diet alone. Others are able to take pills that stimulate their insulin production. But many diabetics cannot survive without daily injections of insulin. However, with proper attention, the otherwise healthy diabetic can live and work in the same way as the nondiabetic.

## Diabetes-Related Problems

A diabetic coma usually occurs as a result of insulin withdrawal, or infection, and is sometimes aggravated by improper diet. An insulin reaction ("insulin shock") appears rapidly, and is much more common than a diabetic coma and is due to a dose of insulin in excess of the body's needs under the circumstances at the time. IF A DIABETIC COMA IS SUSPECTED, IMMEDIATE MEDICAL ATTENTION IS MANDATORY; WITHOUT TREATMENT, A DIABETIC COMA RESULTS IN DEATH.

Fortunately, most diabetics are familiar with their condition, and are concerned about managing their lives in a way that will not aggravate the condition. In addition, most diabetes-related reactions are mild. Every diabetic who takes insulin should have some form of sugar available at all times to take in the event of an insulin reaction.

As a part of the diabetic's regular medical treatment program, food intake should be kept approximately constant from day to day. Some diabetics may receive a "fifth feeding" in the form of a

---

# Distinguishing Insulin Reactions and Diabetic Comas

Correctional officers should be aware of the ways to tell the difference between insulin reaction and diabetic coma:

|  | *Insulin Reaction* | *Diabetic Coma* |
| --- | --- | --- |
| How it Starts | Sudden | Gradual |
| Skin | Pale (may be moist) | Flushed, dry |
| Behavior | Disoriented (confused) | Drowsy |
| Breath | Normal | Fruity odor |
| Breathing | Normal to rapid | Deep, labored |
| Vomiting | Absent | Present |
| Tongue | Moist | Dry |
| Hunger | Present | Absent |
| Thirst | Absent | Present |
| Sugar in urine | Absent or slight | Large amounts |

sack meal to eat in their cell at bedtime to keep their food intake more constant throughout the day.

When an adverse insulin reaction is too rapid for the diabetic to be capable of self-help, sugar in some form should be given immediately. A lump of table sugar, a glass of fruit juice, a piece of candy, or a soft drink can serve the purpose. If the condition is not corrected, the diabetic may lose consciousness entirely. If a diabetic becomes unconscious for any reason, call for medical assistance immediately. A coma can become a serious, or fatal, threat to the life of a diabetic inmate if medical attention is not given immediately. A doctor is best qualified to establish the level of insulin intake.

## Asthma and Other Chronic Illnesses

Inmates with known chronic illnesses frequently present a management dilemma to medical staff as well as to correctional officers and other personnel. In addition to providing for the real medical needs of these individuals, staff must often deal with inmates who may exaggerate their difficulties or fake new symptoms for other nonmedical reasons—special privileges, unwarranted individual attention, excuses from work or other assignments, or even to set the stage for a major security breach. Sometimes the motivation may be only to break the monotony of institutional life, or to cause a disruption.

On the other hand, inmates with legitimate chronic illnesses are also likely to experience significant symptoms, which may result from complications of the basic illness or even the development of new diseases. The problem of telling the difference between real and faked or exaggerated complaints can be quite difficult even for the physician, and especially for the correctional officer. While some judgment must be exercised, the correctional officer should always make a medical referral if there is any reasonable doubt about the need for an inmate to receive medical care. Even a known malingerer may develop a real disease. Correctional officers must avoid premature judgments influenced by an inmate's previous deceptive behavior.

### Asthma Cases

While these concerns should apply to any chronic illness, patients with asthma deserve special mention. These individuals are subject to sudden periodic episodes when the small air passages (bronchial tubes) inside their lungs become closed, causing a failure to inhale enough oxygen. Many such incidents may be mild, and may respond well to prescribed medication, which may be in the patient's possession or available in the living unit. However, in many documented prison experiences, the margin between an apparently

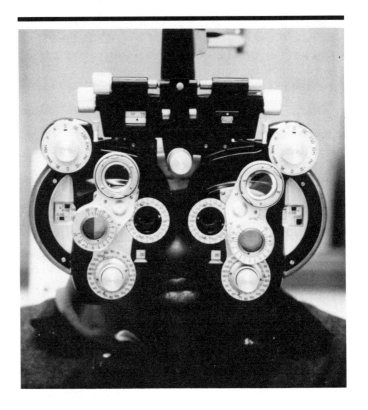

"mild" episode and a significant life-threatening experience can be small and deceptive. Correctional officers should be particularly alert to asthma situations and make early medical referrals.

## Drug Abuse and Addiction

Drug addiction refers to the uncontrollable, usually harmful use of drugs. A drug addict is someone who has a psychological or physical dependence on a chemical substance—a person who needs to experience the "lift" from a drug. There are many substances that can be abused, and each has a different effect on the people who use them; many are highly addictive.

The physical reason for drug addiction is thought to be the body adjusting its pattern of natural chemical use to the presence of the drug, so that it needs the drug to stay in balance; this results in a physical craving for the drug. The psychological reason for addiction is more complicated in many cases, but certainly involves an exaggerated feeling of well-being that taking the drug produces. In such a condition, people feel free from daily anxieties and problems that everyone has. The psychological need for this escape may cause the "cured" addict to return to drugs even after the physical need has been long gone. Addicts can be successfully treated. Unfortunately, most of them get treatment only when forced to by circumstances like prison. In such cases, treatment is less likely to work.

There are many drugs that can be abused; the most common categories are: narcotics, depressants (frequently barbiturates), stimulants (such as amphetamines and cocaine), and hallucinogens (such as LSD and PCP). Marijuana and hashish are also abused drugs, but the degree of psychological and physical dependence they present is not well-established. Drug abusers or addicts often use these drugs in combination, or with alcohol. The abuse of any of these substances presents a serious problem in the institution.

## Symptoms of Drug Use

Whatever the particular substance may be, there are certain signs that may indicate an inmate is using drugs: He or she may act silly; appear drowsy and move slowly; breathe very shallowly or rapidly and deeply; have very small or large pupils; speak slowly or slur speech; stagger or lack coordination; appear excited or overly active; be unable to sleep or concentrate; have little desire for food; and sweat greatly in cool temperatures.

In addition to these physical symptoms, drug addicts using needles frequently can be quickly identified by the presence of punctures and scars on various parts of their body, usually their arms. Many addicts inject drugs directly in the large vein in the arm ("main line") and leave "main line scars" in the crook of their elbow. Large dark tattoos could conceal needle scars.

If drug abuse by an inmate is suspected, the officer should immediately report this to a supervisor and, if practical, detain the inmate. Officers should be aware that extremes of behavior may occur when individuals are under the influence of drugs, and

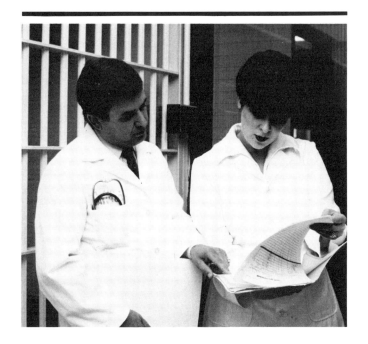

*If drug abuse by an inmate is suspected, the officer should immediately report this to a supervisor and, if practical, detain the inmate.*

should use extreme care and caution when approaching such inmates. Institution policy should be followed if there is a need to subdue an inmate under the influence of drugs.

Known addicts bear close watching because they may go to any length to procure or introduce drugs. The admission physical examination should be particularly thorough, for any body opening might be used to hide a "fix." Incoming mail and all other outside contacts should be scrutinized carefully. Addicts have been known to receive contraband drugs through very unusual methods, such as hidden under the stamps of their mail.

## The Nature of Abused Drugs

Most narcotics are derived from opium. Addiction to them causes an intense physical craving; if addicts do not get their narcotics they develop physical symptoms. Of the opium derivatives, heroin most easily causes addiction, and morphine is a close second. Demerol is another drug with considerable addictive potential. Codeine addiction may also occur but is less severe.

Unlike narcotics (such as morphine, heroin, demerol, and codeine), depressants (such as barbiturates used as sleeping pills) can affect the addicted person's brain and muscle control. Withdrawal symptoms may include anxiety, insomnia, tremors, delirium, convulsions, and possibly death.

In addition to drugs that produce a calming effect (sedatives) such as the opium derivatives and barbiturates, some people become addicted to stimulating drugs (amphetamines) like Benzedrine (called "goof balls"), preludin, cocaine, and others. On the street, the overstimulated, irritable, excited, restless, even psychotic conditions these drugs can cause, as well as the need for money to pay for them, may result in criminal offenses. In the institution, these drugs cause equally serious problem behavior. Withdrawal signs may include apathy, long periods of sleep, irritability, depression, and disorientation.

Hallucinogens (such as LSD and PCP) are drugs that may causes illusions, hallucinations, and poor perception of time and distance. Many PCP users have reacted to its use with acute psychotic episodes or unusually violent behavior that requires large numbers of staff to control, as well as the use of hard or soft restraints. Withdrawal signs have not been reported in the use of hallucinogens, but flashbacks can occur, where the person has signs of drug use for a long time after having used a drug.

It is important to remember that an overdose of narcotics, depressants, stimulants, or hallucinogens can result in death. Medical assistance must be called immediately after finding an unconscious inmate who may have overdosed, so that properly trained individuals can attempt to revive the inmate.

## Alcoholism

The alcoholic's crimes are often committed while under the influence of alcohol. Prolonged, excessive use of alcohol may cause not only criminal behavior, but also physical damage to the brain and other body organs. Some alcoholics experience relatively brief psychotic episodes, with panic and hallucinations (delirium tremens or "DTs"). DTs are actually physical withdrawal symptoms that appear when the alcoholic is unable to get a drink. In such cases, they are in serious need of medical care, because they may become dangerous to themselves or others. More severe alcoholics can develop permanent brain damage with accompanying memory difficulties, or liver damage.

Being in prison or jail for short or even long terms is by itself no cure for alcoholism. Because of the severity of this personality difficulty, treatment of the alcoholic is a long-term procedure. The detoxification process (taking the person off the drug) must be conducted under medical care. In some institutions, qualified medical personnel prescribe medication to ease the withdrawing alcoholic's distress, or even maintain them on a drug that will make them ill if they drink alcohol.

Some specific institutional issues that will be covered in local policy are the actual detoxification process for drunk inmates, the use of small, portable breathalyzer units to establish drunkenness, and the widespread security measures that are in place throughout the institution to search for and detect illegal "brew."

*APPLICABLE ACA STANDARDS*

Medical and Health Care Services: 3-4326 to 3-4379

# 11

## Mentally Ill Inmates

Not all crimes result from mental illness, but many inmates have a background of mental health problems. This section describes the most common types and provides some basic information on how to respond to them in the prison setting.

Most people try to face their problems realistically. Some, though, are unable to, and as a result, they suffer from various types of mental illnesses, and may be diagnosed as having either a neurotic, psychotic, or personality disorder. Each of these categories is recognizable by different symptoms or signs. Correctional officers who carefully observe inmates and see these symptoms should refer them to supervisory, medical, or mental health staff. Officers are not in a position to actually treat mental illnesses, but as will be seen, they are in a key position to help inmates deal with them in the correctional setting.

### Neuroses

Neuroses are ordinarily the mildest form of emotional illness. The neurotic (a person with a neurosis) is extremely anxious and, therefore, unable to deal effectively with reality. The problem is not what these people believe, but rather how they feel: anxious, fearful, and tense. They are often easily upset and continually worried about the future; some may shake and sweat (experience anxiety attacks) or unreasonably fear people, places, or things (express phobias). They may become overly concerned about illnesses, complaining of aches all over, a rundown feeling, or something as specific as a headache, leg pain, upset stomach, or a backache; they may even become temporarily paralyzed or blind. Although a product of the person's mental processes, the neurotic's discomfort is real and should neither be ignored nor rewarded.

Everyone worries unduly about minor things from time to time ("Did I lock the house, turn off the iron, unplug the coffee maker, etc.?"). But for a neurotic person, irrational or unreasonable thoughts—thoughts of harming or committing forbidden acts—make it difficult to communicate with the world. Even though they may never be acted upon, these thoughts are nonetheless very distressing to them.

Just as some neurotics are deeply concerned about irrational ideas, others feel strongly driven to act in unreasonable and unproductive ways. Such a person is called overly compulsive. Although anyone can be compulsive at times (particularly neat or precise when it is not necessary, for instance), compulsions become a problem when they interfere with people's self-esteem and incapacitate them. The uncontrollable desire to set fires (pyromania) or to steal indiscriminately (kleptomania), for instance, are criminal compulsions. Compulsive behaviors or misbehaviors partially ease persistent tension that results from unresolved conflicts. People in this category can be perfectionists, making them excellent workers. Others may be compelled to act out their sexual or aggressive urges in ways they cannot control. Chronically unhappy and sometimes severely depressed neurotics often move and speak slowly. When depressed, these individuals also appear to feel worthless, to have lost their self-respect, and they may become suicidal. Anyone who expresses suicidal ideas should be taken seriously.

### Psychoses

Psychosis is a severe form of mental disturbance in which painfully distorted thoughts and intense emotions disable people (who are called psychotics). Often, they cannot communicate with the real world, and are referred to as "crazy" or "insane." While

application of the laws on insanity varies from state to state, a ruling of insanity in a criminal matter usually relieves a person from responsibility for committing a criminal act, because the person is assumed to have acted out of a mental illness over which he or she had no control.

Some psychotics display distorted thoughts that result in garbled speech that is often difficult to understand. Psychotics may speak rapidly, jumping from thought to thought at such a great rate of speed that the listener is frequently left far behind. Others may talk incoherently, making remarks that do not appear to fit with the topic of conversation, or using words in such a personal way that their meaning is changed. Severely disturbed psychotics occasionally make up their own words.

The distortions in a psychotic's thinking may be accompanied by delusions—unreasonable, false beliefs. Delusions of persecution, for instance, can mean thinking that one is the object of a group plot. Some psychotics have incorrect beliefs that outside objects and situations are connected to them (thinking, for instance, that one is the subject of newspaper stories or television or radio broadcasts, when one is not); people who think their thoughts

and actions are controlled by others suffer from delusions of influence. Those who falsely believe they are unusually skillful, famous, or noteworthy are exhibiting delusions of grandeur. Their ideas can range from mistakenly thinking they are particularly good artists to believing they can read minds, are descendents of distinguished families, or are God.

Psychotics frequently hear, see, feel, taste, or even smell things that are not there (hallucinations). "Hearing voices" is the most frequent form of hallucination. A psychotic homosexual with guilt feelings about sexual impulses might hear voices calling him a "fairy." (However, this does not mean that a homosexual is a psychotic.) Aggressive individuals might hear voices commanding them to commit violent acts. Likewise, psychotics can have visual hallucinations with any type of content, from sexual to religious.

Psychotics' emotional reactions are severely exaggerated or distorted, and can be so severe that the psychotics stop moving or talking. On the other hand, their despair can be so great that they pace, wring their hands, and cry out in suffering and guilt. In some psychotics, "normal" good humor or mood swings are exaggerated and the person becomes "manic"—joking, laughing, talking rapidly, etc. Others fail to exhibit any emotional reaction at all, even during joyous or tragic situations. Still others respond directly opposite of what one would normally expect—laughing over the death of a loved one, or crying when good news is heard. Some even show their mixed emotions by crying and laughing at the same time.

## Personality Disorders

People with personality disorders tend to act out their personal distress, and often get into trouble as a result. Although they are not usually bothered by their own troubles, like the neurotic, psychotic, or even the "normal" person, people with personality disorders typically have difficulty adjusting to life

As the lies become more complex, the antisocial person may have trouble knowing the difference between the real situation and the one he or she made up. Like the "big stories" of normal children and the daydreams of normal adults, these pathological lies usually have a wish-fulfilling quality, in which the liar presents himself or herself as an important person, either as a "conquering hero" or as the long-suffering target of others' abuse and lies. Although they have a callous contempt for others, their pose of reasonableness, friendliness, and warmth may sway people. Some of these individuals are subtle agitators or underminers of authority.

## Personality Trait Disturbances

People with personality trait disturbances show behavior problems that are more the consequence of immediate difficulties. Two of these most noticeable in institutions are the emotionally unstable personality and the passive-aggressive personality.

Emotionally unstable people characteristically lack control. They panic easily in emergencies. They may show explosive tempers. They cannot cope with their own difficulties. Their poor judgment prevents them from forming lasting relationships with other people. They are often genuinely sorry for their misdeeds, and feel guilty and anxious about them.

The passive-aggressive personality includes three subtypes: the passive-dependent, passive-aggressive, and aggressive types.

• *Passive-dependent.* This type of individual acts like a helpless child in human relationships. This person cannot decide what to do in situations without getting advice from many people; he or she attaches to others in a childish way. The passive-dependent personality clings to institutions, agencies, or individuals for emotional support and decision making.

• *Passive-aggressive.* This type is unable to express aggression directly, relying instead on indirect ways of expressing hostility. Passive-aggressive maneuvers in work assignments include willful inefficiency, slowing down, or curious "inability" to understand instructions, even if the person is of average intelligence. Typically, these people pout and shake their head to communicate their disapproval. Firm emotional control is needed in dealing with them because they are skillful in irritating others by their indirect delaying or sabotaging tactics and ill-concealed resistance.

• *Aggressive.* This personality type lacks control over irritations, destructive wishes, and grudges. Outwardly these people appear hostile, but underneath they are basically dependent. Hostility in these cases can be directly expressed either verbally (malicious gossip or name calling) or physically (assaulting or attacking). These people haven't learned

itself and often resort to alcohol, drugs, or criminal behavior.

There are several types of personality disorders, but the most noticeable and widely known is the antisocial personality. These "rebels without a cause" often clash with society, and have lifelong histories of being in legal and other conflicts; they show little ability to learn from their past troubles. They also cannot postpone satisfying their impulses, and instead live only for the pleasure of the moment. Although they may be shrewd planners, their inability to endure tension prevents them from adjusting to routine tasks over a long period of time. Consequently, their work history and institutional adjustment are likely to be erratic and unstable. This type of inmate is apt to blow up in high-pressure situations.

The antisocial person lives by a pattern of showing bravado and taking risks. As a consequence of tending toward extremes, they commit outrageous acts that a sensible person would never consider. Their risk taking makes them dangerous. Some antisocial people are pathological liars, i.e., they lie for the pleasure of lying, for the pleasure of putting something over on someone, or for getting attention or sympathy by a wild story. When confronted by contradictions or by clear evidence of their lies, the antisocial person is likely to casually ignore them.

to express their aggression in a socially acceptable way. Because they lack inner controls, they require firm discipline to prevent aggressive, emotional outbursts. They also need the opportunity to learn some socially acceptable outlets for their aggression, such as the energy-expending activities of hard work or vigorous, supervised recreation.

It is important to remember that these types of people need help from others much more than they are willing to admit. While they must be required to follow rules and regulations, a firm hand should support them in their good behavior and not just bear down on their misbehavior.

### Other Personality Pattern Disturbances

Other types of personality disorders include those of people whose adjustment difficulties have existed since their infancy. They lack the ability to deal with real problems; their ineffective personality characteristics are so deeply ingrained that they can adjust only under supervision. The following is a partial list of types encountered by correctional staff:

• Some individuals of apparently average mental and physical condition are not able to adequately cope with the environment. They appear to lack determination. Unless they have fortunate life circumstances, they end up on the lowest rung of the social ladder, or because of poor judgment, in jail or prison. Lacking positive feelings about themselves, they tend to easily accept institutional life, where no real demands are made on them to be independent adults.

• People with what is called a cyclothymic personality tend to alternate between being depressed and feeling an exaggerated sense of well-being. They tend to be rather friendly, outgoing people who, because of their bubbling energy, can, if they are well organized, put in a good day's work. However, if they optimistically overreach themselves, they can get into legal difficulties. They are identifiable by their dramatic and frequent mood changes.

• People with a schizoid personality are aloof, given to excessive daydreaming, and unassertive. These people avoid getting emotionally involved with others. They are often, but not always, identifiable in correctional institutions by their isolation from other inmates, not so much because they are rejected, but because they prefer to be alone.

• People with paranoid personalities are suspicious of other people and their motives. They characteristically project their own motives of envy, jealousy, and hostility on other people, expecting the worst from others because of their own strong negative feelings. In a correctional institution, paranoid personalities are troublemakers, seizing on petty incidents to "prove" they have been badly used or to show how things have been mismanaged. They are generally vindictive, grudge-bearing people.

## There are several types of personality disorders, but the most noticeable and widely known is the antisocial personality.

Paranoid inmates are frightened people who truly believe they are persecuted, or that someone is out to "get" them. This type of inmate represents a danger to the correctional officer. However, as violence among inmates is not uncommon, an inmate's fears that other inmates are out to "get" him or her may be justified; therefore, such a complaint should not be taken automatically as a sign of mental illness.

## Dealing with Mentally Ill Inmates

Although a psychotic or neurotic person's retreat from the real world may not be obvious at first, his or her ineffectiveness in dealing with it often is. This strange behavior (which the person cannot control, and for which, therefore, he or she may not be responsible), is sometimes incorrectly described as faking or malingering. While the faker can convincingly complain of everything from a headache to fallen arches, the really sick person often lacks the spirit to even be convincing. All statements should, nevertheless, be taken at face value, until the actual condition is confirmed by responsible medical or mental health staff.

It is important to remember that if officers incorrectly handle emotionally disturbed people, treating them as malingerers, these inmates may feel more misunderstood and more upset, and their condition may worsen. Facts about an inmate's behavior, appearance, and attitude, not just opinions, should be noted by officers in order to contribute to an evaluation. How individuals act when they think they are unobserved is particularly important.

### Stages of Mental Deterioration

In identifying the signs of emotional disturbance and mental illness, correctional officers should keep in mind that these stages of mental deterioration often result in the person becoming different—not only from others but also from their usual self. Thus, if an inmate who usually mixes fairly well with others starts to remain alone, fails to come out of the cell even for privileges, goes off in a corner during yard time, or sits and stares into space for hours, that

inmate is referred to them for evaluation.

As individuals vary, so do the illnesses that can be seen in each; there is no one fixed rule for dealing with them in all cases; correctional officers are responsible for using their best judgment. It is important to remember that "chewing out" the inmate or poking fun can do more harm than good. Some individuals need a firm, gentle, and supportive approach. Others could become violently aggressive and might need to be restrained.

If the disturbed inmate who is acting out does not respond to firm, unemotional commands, the correctional officer, keeping in mind the immediate danger of injuries to other inmates or personnel, should try to get assistance. The presence of several officers and medical/mental health personnel may serve to discourage an aggressive inmate from further acting out. A show of force in numbers usually makes the actual use of force unnecessary. In any case, prompt action is mandatory to prevent serious injury to the disturbed inmate, other inmates, or to staff.

person may be showing signs of avoiding the everyday world, or withdrawing.

As they become mentally ill, inmates may become less responsive to daily routine, slowing or becoming erratic at work. Officers need to notice individuals who begin to neglect their appearance—forget to shave, comb their hair, or button their shirt or blouse. Individuals may slow down in speech or actions if becoming depressed; as discussed previously, other disturbed people may begin to talk rapidly or incoherently. Patterns of sleep disturbances can also occur; they may suffer from insomnia or sleep so soundly they do not awaken to morning wakeup calls. They can be apathetic (unresponsive to others) or extremely sensitive and irritated, increasingly lacking control over these feelings. If apathetic, they become indifferent to orders; if irritated, they may angrily refuse to follow them. In responding to orders, they might act confused. Although they may appear willing enough, mentally ill inmates might need to have instructions repeated.

If a correctional officer notices some of these signs of emotional disturbance or any other indications that an inmate's behavior is deteriorating, then a supervisor should be notified. Observations should be recorded for the use of the mental health staff, if the

## The Suicide Risk

Correctional officers should have a high concern for potentially suicidal behavior exhibited by an inmate. In fact, suicidal behavior is probably more likely to occur in the correctional setting than in any other setting.

The reasons for this are many. First, a large percentage of the correctional population is generally thought to have a higher rate of suicide-prone behavior than the "normal" population. For example, in the community, alcoholics, drug addicts, sex offenders, and the antisocial personality all show a relatively high rate of suicidal behavior, and it is not unusual to incarcerate these types of people in correctional facilities.

Second, people are more apt to end up incarcerated during the course of a suicidal crisis than at most other times during their lives. The personal crisis that initiated the suicidal behavior may also have caused that person to be locked up.

Third, the correctional environment can contribute to suicidal behavior. The authoritarian environment, isolation from family and friends, shame of being incarcerated, and basic dehumanizing aspects of being in prison can all lead to a real possibility of suicidal behavior in the correctional setting.

Suicides most frequently occur early during a period of incarceration. Any person with a history of attempting suicide or making threats of a suicidal nature represents a possible danger. In particular, people arrested or convicted for a capital offense may represent a suicide risk, even though no suicidal statements or gestures may have been made. Even if the inmate's statements sound unreal, they should be taken seriously. No matter how attention-seeking the person may seem to be, acts, gestures, or statements reflecting suicidal intent must be taken seriously. Even though an inmate only seems to be threatening suicide, close surveillance is warranted, and an immediate referral to the appropriate supervisor or medical staff is indicated.

There are many reasons for attempting or threatening suicide, but an obvious one is that the person feels that life has become hopeless. Attempting or committing suicide is not necessarily a psychotic act. Sociopaths and other persons with character disorders are likely to make impulsive, rather than well-planned, suicide attempts.

Some inmates set up suicide attempts to gain staff attention; others mutilate themselves or swallow unusual objects to accomplish the same thing. Unfortunately, many of these gestures can unintentionally turn into a fatal act.

### Policy and Procedures

Every institution should have a specific policy that describes the procedures to be followed when a potentially suicidal inmate is identified; officers should be aware of these policies and review them frequently. Procedures ordered by supervisory, mental health, or medical staff may include a suicide watch, surveillance by closed-circuit television, intensive counseling, or medication.

In the case of a suicide attempt, the officer finding the victim must make a basic decision—whether to summon help first or to try to save the person. In housing areas where the inmates are locked in their cells, the first action should be to get additional staff in the unit—the risk is too great of the "suicide" actually being a setup to get the door open and take over the unit. In less secure settings, the choices are not as clear, but the rule of thumb is to always have backup coming before attempting to assist an inmate in such a situation.

The correctional officer has a responsibility to minimize the chance that an inmate will commit suicide. However, officers should also know that suicides do occur—prevention of 100 percent of all jail and prison suicides is virtually impossible. Officers must remember that they are not responsible for an inmate's suicide; the inmate made a personal decision to commit the act as a way of handling an unhappy or frustrating life situation. However, officers must be aware of suicide prevention information, and actually practice precautionary measures that will minimize the chance of this type of tragedy occurring unnecessarily.

## The Mentally Retarded

The mentally ill person suffers from some form of disrupted functioning of their otherwise normal minds. The mentally retarded, however, are unable to adequately cope with life problems due to their below-average intellectual ability—they simply do not have the mental capacity to function normally.

Many inmates test low on intelligence tests, but this may be a cultural factor, reflecting poor test-taking skills or a lack of facts about today's society; they may nevertheless be "street smart." However, the mentally retarded person lacks a certain basic mental capacity, and therefore cannot deal with the world in a normal way. To complicate matters, there are different degrees of retardation, and mentally retarded people can also become mentally ill.

*Suicidal behavior is probably more likely to occur in the correctional setting than in any other setting.*

Some mentally retarded inmates are incapable of learning to deal effectively with the world in an independent fashion. They are suggestible, and may be easily led into crimes. They are easy "marks" for the shrewd operator, and need to be protected. They may be victimized in the correctional setting in any number of ways, such as sexual assault or pressure or holding or running drugs.

Ideally, mentally retarded individuals should not be housed in prisons; unfortunately, some are. When identified, every effort should be made to place these individuals in an appropriate noncorrectional setting. In the meantime, officers should deal patiently and firmly with mentally retarded inmates, recognizing their limitations. Communications with them must be clear, stated one step at a time. Some are capable of learning to work in routine, supervised tasks. They

*The presence of several officers and medical/mental health personnel may serve to discourage an aggressive inmate from further acting out.*

should not be placed in work situations that demand more of them than their basic ability permits. It may be necessary to place them in a separate housing area or even in a locked unit.

Whatever their intellectual limitations may be, the mentally retarded inmate is entitled to the same respect that any other person would get. These inmates should be protected from the contempt of staff or the ribbing of fellow inmates.

## Medication and Treatment

The treatment of each of these conditions is far too complicated to spell out in this publication. Mental health and medical staff are responsible for deciding the best course of action in each individual case. They also are responsible for seeing that correctional staff are aware of the specific problem cases in the institution population, and the best day-to-day strategies for managing them.

Group and individual counseling is used with some inmates. However, in many instances, it is beyond the institution's resources to provide the intense therapy thought to be necessary to treat many of these difficult cases. The most severe cases should be referred for confinement in a mental health treatment facility.

For some conditions, medications are available to help the inmate control the problem behavior or to function more normally. Medication is not a certain cure, nor a permanent one. Inmates on medication should still be closely observed by staff, and they should be monitored to be sure they keep taking their medicine.

One point of clarification in the area of mental health staff may be useful—the difference between a psychologist and a psychiatrist. A psychologist is a trained professional mental health worker who often has earned a doctorate degree in clinical psychology and specializes in treating people with some type of emotional or mental disturbance. A psychiatrist is a medical doctor who has received additional training specific to the treatment of people with mental health problems. A psychiatrist can prescribe medication for patients, while a psychologist may not.

## Summary

Officers need to be aware of inmate problems stemming from mental health conditions, and to know basic ways of dealing with these problems from an operational standpoint.

Correctional officers are not responsible for diagnosing and treating inmates' special problems. However, because officers work so closely with inmates, their observations can be very useful to those who are responsible for diagnosing and treating them.

*APPLICABLE ACA STANDARDS*

Medical and Health Care Services: 3-4326 to 3-4379

# 12

# Reception, Orientation, and Classification of Inmates

New inmates arrive at the institution after a series of what most people would consider very disturbing events. They have been arrested, detained, tried in court, convicted of a crime, and committed to prison. Well-organized reception and orientation programs lessen inmates' shock at being confined and hasten adjustment to institutional living.

## Reception Activities

The importance of thorough intake processing cannot be overstated. The primary focus is to properly identify and search inmates and all incoming personal property. In some institutions, after this initial intake processing, newly admitted inmates are placed in a quarantine section for 10 days to two weeks, where they undergo thorough physical examinations, including blood tests, X-rays, inoculations, and vaccinations. A complete social history may be taken at this stage, including information about the inmates, their families, and other pertinent background facts.

Officers assigned to the receiving area perform many, if not all, of the following duties:

- Determine that the individual is legally committed to the institution
- Assign a register number to the inmate
- Completely search the individual and his or her possessions, paying particular attention to all clothing items—seams or cuffs on trouser legs, waistbands, zippers, small (watch) pockets, and all other pockets
- Mark contraband (weapons, narcotics, alcohol,

etc.) properly, and process it according to institutional policy
- Dispose of all medications the inmate arrives with, following established institutional procedures
- Issue an appropriate receipt for any funds in the inmate's possession, and properly store the money in a secure area
- Appropriately search all property and dispose of forbidden personal property by storing it or shipping it to someone in the community, noting any damaged property on an inventory form
- Issue clean, properly fitted clothing, as needed
- Arrange shower and hair care for the inmate, if necessary
- Photograph and fingerprint the inmate, noting on a form any marks or other unusual physical characteristics
- Arrange medical, dental, and mental health screening
- Assign the inmate to a housing area
- Record personal data and information about the inmate to be used to create mail and visiting lists and explain procedures for mail and visiting
- Help inmates notify next of kin and families of their arrival and the institution's address
- Give written orientation materials to new inmates
- Make an immediate decision on whether the inmate has any enemies or persons from whom he or she should be separated in the institution, and take appropriate steps to safeguard the inmate if needed

Many of these same functions are also performed when an inmate is released. Inmates are properly

identified, release authorizations are verified, inmates and property are thoroughly searched, and funds are issued, if authorized.

## Admission and Orientation

Admission and orientation programs usually last about two weeks for transfer cases, and up to a month for new commitments. These programs often include classes, reviews of rules and regulations, and discussions about institutional programs and procedures. New inmates may be allowed to work, read, exercise, and attend religious services according to the same schedule as the general inmate population. In some states orientation programs may be conducted in the quarantine area.

During the admission and orientation process, staff should:

- Explain institutional rules and regulations, provide a written copy of those materials (translated into the inmate's language, if necessary), and have the inmate sign a form that he or she received the inmate handbook
- Describe available programs, their goals, and how inmates are accepted into them
- Administer tests that identify special interests, talents, or problems
- Provide general help for inmates in the transition into institutional living
- Document that the inmate has completed all phases of the orientation program

Naturally, new inmates are unfamiliar with institution rules and staff expectations. During the orientation process, staff members explain to new inmates, as well as those transferred from other institutions, how the prison operates and what will be expected of them.

During orientation, new inmates may be taken on a guided tour of the institution and then interviewed by representatives from the educational, industrial, custodial, recreational, and religious departments. During this period, inmates may be examined by the medical staff, tested by the psychologist, and interviewed by a psychiatrist, counselor, or caseworker, who may discuss the inmate's health, family, and personal problems.

This evaluation process is vital, because the inmate's adjustment to prison is largely affected by these factors. The early days of imprisonment are difficult for inmates, particularly first offenders, who are getting the "feel" of the institution. In some prisons, counselors or caseworkers are involved in orienting the individual to the program; in others the unit officer has that responsibility. Three goals of orientation are: (1) to familiarize inmates with the institution's expectations; (2) give staff an opportunity to learn more about the inmate for classification purposes; and (3) help inmates feel that someone is interested in helping them adjust.

At the end of the admission and orientation program, the information gathered by the staff is forwarded to the institution's classification committee or a unit team for use in the classification process.

## Special Intake Cases

Some inmates require special handling immediately upon arrival in the institution. While local procedures for these cases will differ, it is important to mention the most common types:

• *Suicide Risks.* The first hours and days of a new inmate's prison experience can be filled with fear and tension. For some, the humiliation of imprisonment is almost unbearable; for others, pressures from other inmates can be overwhelming. Correctional staff in orientation and receiving areas should be very alert to the signs of depression or pre-suicidal behavior mentioned in Chapter 11 of this guide. Staff should be trained in the policy and procedures for handling potentially suicidal inmates and providing proper supervision and care.

• *Protective Custody Cases.* When inmates come into

the institution and declare themselves to be needing protective custody, or when reliable information is received that a new inmate may be in danger, the intake or admission and orientation staff should be prepared to take special supervision and security precautions until the degree of risk is evaluated and the inmate is removed, if necessary, to a safe, secure area.

• *Medical Isolation Cases* (perhaps including AIDS cases). Each institution will have medical standards for screening and isolating incoming cases. These standards ordinarily require intake staff to immediately notify medical personnel if an incoming inmate displays or reports any key symptom or medical history. Immediate transfer to the institution hospital is usually followed by a modified orientation program conducted there, rather than in the orientation unit. In correctional systems that house AIDS patients separately, an orientation program is often conducted right in the AIDS unit.

• *Special Management or High-Security Cases.* These high-risk escape or violent inmates are often identified in advance as ultra-high-security cases. For them, the processing must involve extra staff, perhaps the use of restraints, and in most cases, a modified orientation program conducted for them while they are in a locked unit. Staff safety and institutional security must be the first concerns in handling these cases.

• *Parole Violators.* These inmates may have returned to the institution for a violation hearing, or following such a hearing. If they have been in the institution before, a shortened orientation program is often used.

## Classification Procedures

Classifying inmates is not, as some believe, simply separating inmates into different types and assigning them to institutions. Classification is a multistage process designed to fulfill three objectives: (1) to assess inmates' backgrounds and behavior in order to assign them to appropriately secure institutions and to appropriate levels of supervision; (2) to develop a program plan with each inmate, based on a prior assessment; and (3) to make certain that each inmate's progress is periodically evaluated and, if necessary, modify the program and custody level.

Proper classification ensures that inmates are confined in the least restrictive, appropriate facility without presenting an undue risk to the public, staff, or other inmates. Inmates should not receive more

surveillance, or be kept in a more secure institution, than required by the level of risk they present. Keeping inmates of generally the same level of security and aggressiveness in one institution greatly reduces the likelihood of serious management problems (as opposed to a situation where weak and strong, high-escape and low-escape risk cases are all together).

### Classification Approaches

Classification can be handled in several ways. In some correctional systems, all new inmates are sent to a reception and diagnostic facility where staff from various specialty areas (such as psychology, health services, social services, and education) interview, test, and evaluate each inmate. From the information they gather, staff decide where to send the inmate to serve the initial part of the sentence as well as the programs the inmate needs. In other systems, cases are pre-screened using probation or other court documents, and the decision on where to send the inmate is made while he or she is still in the jail or on bond. In some small systems, where only one institution serves an entire state, the inmates are simply sent to the institution's reception and diagnostic unit and, while there, evaluated for housing and custody.

In these latter two cases, the classification team (or in some cases a unit team) begins by analyzing the problems presented by each individual. The team reviews inmates' criminal, social, and medical histories; studies individuals' psychiatric/psychological examinations; and evaluates their vocational, religious, and recreational backgrounds. In most systems, the inmates participate in this process by assessing their own needs and, to a degree, selecting programs to meet those needs.

This analysis for classification purposes can be done in one of several ways. Traditionally,

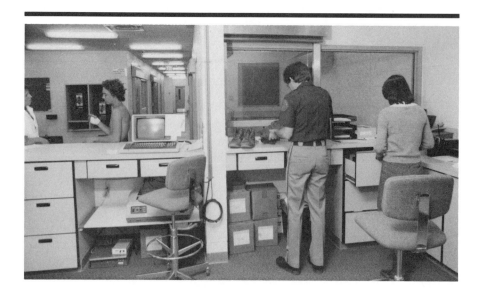

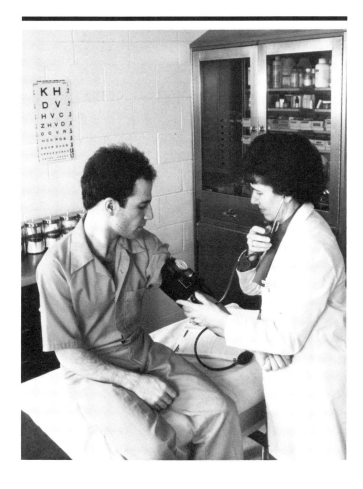

## Proper classification ensures that inmates are confined in the least restrictive, appropriate facility without presenting an undue risk to the public, staff, or other inmates.

classification committees have reviewed the available information, and based on their professional, subjective judgment (that is, not using any fixed or predefined rules) decided the inmates' institutional destination (if transfer is an option), custody classification, housing assignment, job, and programs.

In more sophisticated systems, however, the committee or unit team reviews a set of predetermined factors to help staff make these decisions. In some cases, agency staff gather the court information in advance and evaluate it using a security scoring form to decide where the inmate will be initially confined. When an inmate arrives at the designated institution, the additional information gathered during orientation is used to make any adjustments in assignment, as well as for other internal management decisions.

The advantage of this latter system is that it is consistent. It removes the element of personal bias from the classification process. The best systems allow staff to override a numerically determined score if, in their professional judgment, the inmate requires more or less security than the form indicates; the reasons for such overrides must be documented.

There also are classification approaches that subdivide prison populations to improve internal management, but a detailed description of them is beyond the scope of this publication. Generally they

serve the same purpose—to keep inmates with similar behavior characteristics in the same housing units, where they get along better with each other than if mixed with all other types of individuals.

### Classification Policies

No matter which system is used, classification policies must include, at a minimum:

- A description of the membership of the unit, team, or institutional classification committee(s), as well as the duties and responsibilities of each member
- Detailed descriptions of procedures for classifying and reclassifying inmates, and for documenting the results of the process
- Procedures for transferring inmates from one program to another, or from one institution to another
- Provision for a transcript or some other record of the classification or team action on every case; these records can help parole authorities evaluate whether an inmate can or should return to the community

### Classification Committees

Who is on the committee? The makeup of the classification committee or unit team depends, of course, on the staff available. Members of classification teams are generally department heads and specialists concerned primarily with diagnosis, training, treatment, and custody of the inmates. They may be associate wardens in charge of treatment or custody, supervisors of classification, education, and vocational training, and/or the head social worker or sociologist. The chief medical officer, counselor, psychiatrist, psychologist, chaplain, and officers in charge of the admission and orientation unit may also sit on the committee.

Large institutions must avoid establishing large committees that occupy the time of too many staff members. Where the classification and reclassification load is heavy, it may be necessary to form a

unit psychologist, and unit officer. This group is responsible for making almost all of the initial and reclassification decisions regarding inmates, including recommendations for parole.

Correctional officers who maintain accurate records can make a valuable contribution to the classification process. The information contained in them is used by classification committees and unit teams to make vital decisions concerning inmates.

## Summary

The way that inmates are received and classified can affect their institutional adjustment during confinement. During this initial process, staff assess inmates, assign them, and work with them to develop program plans. Proper admission, orientation, and classification procedures help correctional officers by ensuring that inmates are properly screened, are confined in appropriate facilities, know the rules, and are aware of the programs that best meet their needs.

*APPLICABLE ACA STANDARDS*

Classification: 3-4282 to 3-4293
Reception and Orientation: 3-4272 to 3-4281

subcommittee to handle this process. Conversely, in institutions with limited staff, one committee member may assume the functions ordinarily carried out by members from more than one department.

Whether there is one or more classification committees, it is important that the committee represent each service or department so that an accurate profile of the inmate is established and a well-rounded program devised.

### Unit Teams

Who is on the unit team? In an institution that uses unit management, the unit team handles almost all of the functions of the classification committee. The team ordinarily consists of the unit manager, case manager, counselor, unit education representative,

# 13

## Programming and Related Services

For most of the history of corrections in America, the idea of institutional programs meant only the activity necessary to maintain custody of inmates, and perhaps some simple work for them. As thinking about the causes of crime gradually changed, ideas about institutional programs also changed. Now it is generally believed that in a much broader sense, programs are an important part of any institution's operation and even its security.

Correctional institutions today are geared to protecting society first, and to providing a safe, humane place to confine inmates—a place where they can find the resources to change their lives if they want to. Officers are primarily responsible for the first part of this goal, providing secure, safe confinement. But even in the last area—providing opportunities for change—officers can help.

### Program Models

First, some background is helpful. For many years corrections used a model for its "treatment" programs called "the medical model." This involved assuming that professionally trained staff could identify the causes of inmates' criminal behavior, and tell the inmate how to change through participating in certain programs, just as a medical doctor diagnoses a patient's illness and prescribes medicine or other treatment to cure the condition. Criminal behavior was thought to be curable in that way, and long-range "treatment" was intended to send offenders back into the community as useful, law-abiding citizens for the rest of their lives.

This opinion is less widely held now than in the past, although there are many staff who still think this is a sound approach to prison management, and many excellent programs still operate on this basis.

However, now the institution's responsibility is more commonly thought to be to provide the broadest possible range of program options for inmates, to steer them to those that appear to deal with any basic needs they have (such as educational or vocational training), and then to let the inmates decide whether to participate or not.

The underlying thought here is that, "You can lead a horse to water, but you can't make it drink." Put directly, there is no way for institution staff to force inmates to change if they do not want to, and there are some inmates who very plainly do not want to change. For them, most correctional professionals believe that protection of society is a valid reason for confinement, and the job of correctional staff is limited to providing safe, humane conditions of confinement. This is not to say that counseling and other support services are not important, but for many corrections professionals, the time of prescribed "treatment" is largely gone.

Fortunately, the days of the custody/treatment disagreements are largely over. Most program staff realize that effective programs cannot exist in a disorderly, dangerous institution. Most correctional staff understand that offering a variety of institutional programs actually helps them manage the institution more effectively. In, short, these two main segments of the institutional community need each other.

Finally, it is also important to note another trend, the movement toward ensuring equal program opportunities for female inmates. In the past, institutions have not provided the same range of programs and services to female inmates as to males. In the face of other, broader trends in society, and an increasing number of court cases on this point, correctional agencies are making equivalent programs available for more and more female inmates.

Given these facts, what should an institution do?

## Programs are an important part of any institution's operation and even its security.

What programs are realistic and important to have? Which ones really address inmates' needs?

In fact, there is much for institutions to do, and programs are valuable in the prison setting. Inmates typically are educationally and vocationally unprepared for functioning in today's society. They often have poorly developed social and interpersonal skills. There are many ways that personal change can prepare inmates to function lawfully upon return to society, if they want to. And it is in those areas that institutions are focusing their efforts.

## Social or Casework Services

Society demands that correctional institutions provide more than security and public safety. Society places a high value on providing inmates with the opportunity to make steps toward some form of personal change, popularly called rehabilitation.

To assist in providing these services, most institutions provide a social service, classification, guidance, or unit team system. By whatever name it is known, the responsibility of these casework staff is to plan an ongoing, individualized program for each inmate.

ACA standards describe a system that ensures inmates receive attention to their individual needs, in which each is assigned to a counselor or member of a unit management team. In this way, each inmate can be assured access to at least one employee for advice and assistance. This person is expected to maintain continuing personal contact with the inmate.

Employees assigned to full-time casework or counseling positions should have sufficient training and experience to provide guidance that will be responsive to inmates' needs. Correctional officers or other untrained staff who work closely with inmates may, nonetheless, provide informal counseling on institutional adjustment issues.

Ordinarily, each caseworker has a caseload, like that of a parole officer in the community. Once an inmate is assigned to a particular caseworker, the inmate remains his or her responsibility until released from the institution. This caseworker does not act in the place of the classification committee or unit team (which has the overall responsibility for developing an inmate's program). The caseworker, instead, has responsibilities to provide individual services to the inmate and to meet the administrative and organizational needs of the institution in the casework area.

The caseworker should make all nonconfidential file material available to staff who have a legitimate need to know the information contained in the file. These files are maintained for effective institution administration, for planning an overall program for each individual, and for compiling necessary reports for the paroling authority and other agencies. The correctional officer needing additional information to more effectively supervise any particular inmate usually can secure such information from the caseworker. However, all file information, even that released as nonconfidential within the institution, is still restricted in terms of any release outside the facility.

The caseworker is usually responsible for planning and coordinating the inmate's program, as well as helping the inmate adjust to institutional life. The average inmate has numerous problems. Difficulty in abiding by the law is a major one, but in many instances inmates also have trouble adjusting to institutional routines. In addition, any problems that involve family at home, or community activity affecting the inmate, are the general responsibility of the caseworker.

Correctional officers should exercise care when discussing an inmate's problems. If the matter deals strictly with institutional procedures, correctional officers certainly can discuss it. However, when faced with noninstitutional concerns, correctional officers should refer the inmate to the official whose responsibility covers that particular function.

In order to be available to help inmates with their personal problems and with adjustment to the institution, casework staff should be available on a regularly scheduled basis for appointments requested by inmates. Because inmates may have problems that require immediate attention, at least one professional staff member should be available at all times, either on-site or on immediate call. In most locations, some members of the unit staff or other program staff are available during the hours when inmates are permitted out of their cells. Other crisis intervention services should be available on an as-needed basis to assist more seriously disturbed inmates, through a medical or mental health duty officer system.

# Education

Educational programs often assume special importance in correctional facilities. Many inmates' educational backgrounds are seriously deficient; many inmates lack a high school diploma, and many others have less than a sixth-grade education.

A sound institutional education program should provide a well-rounded general education. It should offer a variety of programs including the following: the Adult Basic Education (ABE) Program, for inmates who have not attained a sixth-grade education; the General Education Development (GED) program, so that inmates can work toward their high school equivalency diploma; a postsecondary education program for those who have successfully completed high school and want to further their education; and continuing education courses for those who want to update their skills and knowledge.

## Education Staff

The education department staff usually consists of a full-time program administrator, assistant, and clerk, as well as instructors specializing in ABE, GED, college-level courses, and continuing education programs. Frequently, the full-time education staff are supplemented by contract staff, who enrich the standard programs and offer special courses as the need arises. Education options should be broad enough to provide for the needs, interests, and abilities of as many inmates as possible. In institutions with a significant number of non-English-speaking inmates, for example, courses in English as a second language may be necessary.

Close working relationships among educational and classification or unit team personnel are essential. Education in the correctional setting is ideally considered part of a total program, and a proper balance should be maintained between academic and vocational training and recreation. Emphasis should be placed on developing programs that will deal with individual educational needs; special attention should be paid to the needs of inmates who are unusually far behind in key areas, such as reading.

## Developing an Educational Program

The process of developing an educational program should include input from the inmate involved, and a follow-up system should be developed to regularly review program progress. Counseling should be available to provide inmates assistance, encouragement, and feedback with respect to their educational and vocational goals.

Teaching in a correctional setting requires a certain breed of professional. Inmates who have failed throughout life in various learning experiences, and particularly in the classroom setting, are a very difficult group to control and motivate. Meeting the educational needs of inmates requires a thorough knowledge of their individual learning problems.

The staff/inmate ratio is another significant factor influencing effectiveness in any teaching environment. Inmates in general require at least the same, and in many cases more, interaction, feedback, and personal attention than that provided students in outside educational programs. This is, in part, because inmates vary greatly in learning ability, interest level, and motivation. The educational program should be structured so that inmates can enter at any time, and proceed through the various grades at their own pace. Progress through the program should not be defined by grade level attainment, academic marks, or scores; individualized instruction is essential. Programmed instruction teaching machines, correspondence courses, and educational television may be used, in addition to traditional teaching methods. In some institutions, the education department also provides courses in consumer activities, life skills, and family life.

Education programs should not compete with work assignments, visitation, counseling, and other activities, but should be offered at nonpeak program hours, and should be available in the evenings and on weekends. Participation can be encouraged by limiting the barriers to attendance; some systems even use a reward system.

Recognition of academic and vocational achievements, in the form of certification or graduation ceremonies, is helpful to individual inmates, and enhances the general support for educational programs. The ceremonies also can be used to good effect in a public information program to highlight the institution's successes.

## Vocational Training

The primary goal of vocational training is to provide inmates with marketable skills so they are better equipped to earn a living for themselves and their dependents when released to the community.

Traditional trades, such as carpentry, plumbing, welding, painting, automotive repair, and electrical work are usually taught in the facility's maintenance shops and supplemented by classroom instruction. Separate vocational training space may be used to teach other trades such as computer programming, computer-related equipment operation and repair, and repair of small engines, office equipment, refrigerators, air conditioners, and televisions.

The vocational training program is usually supervised by the education department. The number of full-time instructors varies according to the number of shop areas. Part-time contract employees from a local vocational school can often be hired to help the regular staff. Using contract employees also allows greater flexibility when program modifications are needed in response to changes in the job market.

Vocational training programs should relate to the job market. The community's employment needs can be assessed through contacts with local labor and industry representatives. Equipment and curricula for the vocational training programs should be updated periodically to ensure compatibility with training developments in the community. Existing community resources and community involvement should be used where appropriate. A variety of training areas is often developed this way, in cooperation with other departments such as correctional industries.

Many vocational training programs are linked to outside trades through formal apprenticeship programs in which the inmate completes a very long, detailed course of training and on-the-job experience. The best of these programs prepare inmates to start well-paying jobs upon release. Other, less formal

programs can be used as a springboard to entry-level jobs in the community, because they provide the necessary fundamental training and experience needed to at least break into the field.

## Work Programs

The mission of work programs in a correctional facility is to employ inmates in constructive activities, foster good work habits, and provide training opportunities in a variety of marketable skills. By providing employment opportunities, a work program also reduces the idleness otherwise inherent in correctional facilities. An institution for 500 inmates can often employ as much as 50 percent of its inmate population in an industrial production program. Good work habits, on-the-job training, and even the satisfaction of a day's work well done are a few intangibles that, in the long run, can help change attitudes and behavior.

Work activities can include:

• *Day-to-day services to maintain an institution*, such as food service, routine cleaning, and other housekeeping chores, and maintenance and other services. These routine tasks are relatively simple, and can provide employment opportunities for some inmates. Appropriately classified inmates are frequently assigned to maintenance work outside the institution as members of construction or ground details.

• *Vocational training* in cooking and baking, meat-cutting, power and filtration plant operations, maintenance and repair of refrigeration equipment, automotive maintenance and repair, carpentry, plumbing, painting, bricklaying, sheet metal work, installation of electrical equipment, and some

assignments in the laundry, dry cleaning, and clothing repair plants.

• *Agricultural work and other activities related to farming* such as dairying, poultry raising, and canning. These assignments also serve to reduce institutional food costs by contributing to the supply of meats and vegetables consumed in the institution. Surplus agricultural and dairy products may also yield a financial profit when sold to other public institutions and eligible agencies.

• *Work camps* may be used for inmates who are approaching the end of their sentences or who have relatively short, nonviolent sentences. They provide opportunities for inmates to live and work in an environment that more nearly resembles conditions existing in free communities. Inmates assigned to camps are often employed in construction and repair of roads, reforestation, gardening, harvesting, maintenance and improvement of public park areas, and other work concerned with the conservation of natural resources and the upkeep of public properties. Camp programs for properly screened low-risk inmates can provide a relatively inexpensive option for the relief of overcrowding and idleness in larger institutions.

• *Industrial production.* Correctional industries furnish jobs for inmates who otherwise might be unassigned, or be assigned to jobs that offer no chance to develop marketable skills. Prison industries are often limited to selling their goods to other state agencies, so that they do not compete with private production of similar goods in the open market. Private industries that have been introduced in some correctional facilities provide a realistic work environment for inmates to learn and improve work skills and handle many of the same responsibilities that those in the community work force do. Industrial programs offer both economic profit to the institution and specialized vocational training and experience for the individual inmate.

## Counseling

While correctional officers may provide common-sense advice to inmates, and offer a valuable service when they do, most formal counseling programs are conducted by specialized staff. Correctional staff should not attempt to conduct any in-depth counseling.

Individual sessions with staff members can be effective, as can group therapy sessions. In the institutional setting, where staff resources are short, group counseling is far more common. Staff who are qualified to counsel generally include psychiatrists, psychologists, social workers, caseworkers, and trained lay counselors. The type of counseling programs available to inmates varies greatly, and for

that reason, this chapter will not go into detail on the different methods used.

## Recreation and Inmate Activities

A sound recreational program is a crucial element in any correctional facility. By providing inmates with a constructive means for channeling energies and relieving tension, recreation contributes to the facility's safe and orderly operation. Recreational activities also give inmates an opportunity to use their free time constructively, improve their physical and mental health, and develop good sportsmanship and morale.

Typically, the recreation program consists of a wide variety of organized group and individual activities, including various sports, music, drama, movies, arts and crafts, and table games. Full-time recreation specialists usually coordinate the program, with assistance from security staff and carefully selected inmates. In addition, many community groups and individual volunteers contribute substantial time and effort to help coordinate programs and increase the variety of activities for inmates.

No particular recreational program can be a standard for all institutions; each differs in size,

# Society places a high value on providing inmates with the opportunity to make steps toward some form of personal change, popularly called rehabilitation.

programs, type of population, locale, and physical characteristics. A program that meets the needs of one institution may be a far cry from those in other institutions. Many institutions are limited in the recreational activities they can provide, due to lack of facilities or absence of necessary funds. Wherever the institution or whatever the recreation activity, the resources available must be used to meet the needs of as many inmates as possible. Qualified volunteers can be very helpful in developing and delivering programs, even with limited resources.

## Typical Recreation Facilities

Typical recreation facilities include an outdoor recreation area, or yard; a gymnasium with seats for spectators; an auditorium with stage equipment; game rooms and games such as table tennis, shuffleboard, chess, checkers, and cards; weight-lifting and other body-conditioning equipment and space for their use; a music room; and space for the pursuit of arts, crafts, and hobbies. Locker rooms, showers, and dressing rooms also should be available. Provision should be made for the regular inspection of all equipment, and for repair and replacement as necessary. The National Recreation and Park Association provides guidelines for facilities and equipment, and ACA standards provide an excellent set of guidelines for the types of recreation that should be available.

Recreation should be available during nonworking hours. This affords each inmate opportunity to participate on a voluntary basis. Some provision should be made for inmates with odd work schedules, such as morning watch powerhouse workers, to have access to the recreation facilities during their off-duty hours.

Community interaction can include bringing in volunteers to provide instruction, and inviting local teams to compete with institution teams. It also may include taking low-security inmates into the community for recreational activities.

Movies are provided in most institutions; some provide one or two movies a week, with a special program on holidays. These are often made available through the profits of the canteen or institution store. Institutions also extensively use 16 mm films in the

school's education programs. Video-taped movies are gaining popularity in smaller unit settings.

The library also rates high among recreational outlets for the institution. ACA standards set requirements for institutional library operations. The materials selected must meet inmates' educational, informational, and recreational needs. They should be easily accessible and regulated by a system that prevents abuse.

The institution's library service should be generally comparable to that of a public library, providing logical organization of materials for convenient circulation to satisfy users' needs. Many libraries go so far as to offer information services to locate facts as needed; a reader's advisory service that helps provide suitable materials for users; and even promotion of library materials through publicity, book lists, special programs, book and film discussion groups, music programs, contests, and other appropriate means. The reference collection is very important, particularly when inmates need specialized pre-release, vocational, and educational information.

Hobby and craft work is encouraged in most correctional institutions. Approved projects can include various types of weaving, sewing, leather work, stamp collecting, watch repairing, woodworking, and the making of plaster figurines. In many locations, this kind of activity offers inmates the opportunity to earn money through the sale of products at the institutional store.

Other recreation activities can include:

• Music
• Entertainment by outside groups
• Variety programs by the inmates
• Institution publications
• Holiday events
• Radio
• Television

## Religious Services

Most administrators and wardens in the correctional field understand the importance of religious programs in correctional institutions. ACA standards address the religious issue by emphasizing that all inmates have the right to voluntary exercise of their religious beliefs, when those practices do not interfere with the order and security of the institution. In most facilities, either a full-time chaplain or representative of a faith group from the community should be available to provide regular religious services, individual and group counseling, family contacts, and other services. The chaplain or staff religious program coordinator should see that volunteer religious groups from the community have access to the population, when requested. Inmates should be kept informed about opportunities to participate in religious programs on a continuing basis.

Correctional staff must be sensitive to the increase in the number of less traditional religions found in prison. Many correctional staff have not had the experience of dealing with Islam or other religions that are less well-known in the United States.

Nevertheless, the right of a Muslim inmate to have a *kufi* (a particular type of headpiece) is just as well-established as that of a Jewish inmate to have a *yarmulke*, or a Baptist to have a Bible. The right of a native American to worship in a sweat lodge is becoming just as well recognized as that of a Catholic to attend mass. Correctional agencies are dealing with more of these situations every day, and it is the agency's responsibility to make very clear the policy on how these groups are to be permitted to worship. For the line officer, when in doubt, ask for advice from a supervisor.

### *Chaplains' Functions*

In most institutions, one or more chaplains coordinate religious services and develop community resources to meet the religious needs of all inmates. In most systems, the chaplains have the endorsement of a recognized religious organization. The chaplain's various functions, common to all denominations, include:

• Offering sacramental ministries, including regular religious services and special services connected with baptisms, confessions, communion, etc.
• Coordinating ministries to other faith groups through the use of contracts, lay ministers, and volunteers.
• Providing religious instruction to inmates in the fundamentals of the denomination of which they are a part, and providing instructional resources for other denominations.
• Providing private and personal counseling—an essential part of the chaplain's work that includes interviews in the chaplain's offices and visits to inmates in the hospital, locked units, etc.
• Ministering to inmates' families and other concerned people. Many of the tensions in an institution stem from inmates' worries about the

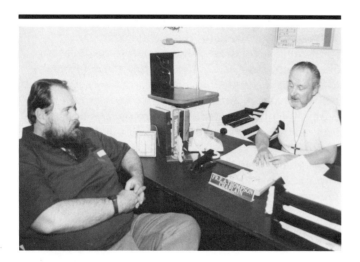

welfare of loved ones, or from the fear that they are being forgotten by people on the outside. A good portion of the chaplain's counseling time addresses these problems.

• Serving as a pastor, guide, and counselor to the institution's employees, as well as the inmates.

• Providing an interpretative ministry to the community. Too often, society views correctional institutions as merely a place to confine people who have violated the law. Chaplains are uniquely equipped to explain the purposes of modern correctional institutions to the community at large, and to enlist their cooperation in the objectives of current correctional procedures.

In their work, chaplains try to help inmates deal with personal problems and the issues of confinement that may lead to positive personal change. Chaplains of all denominations enjoy the confidence of inmates to a degree possessed by no official of the institution, and they try to use this confidence to promote the best interests of the individual and of the institution. This confidentiality is sometimes difficult for other staff to understand; often it is a burden to the chaplain, but it is an essential part of their role, and staff and inmates should respect it.

## Officers' Relation to Religious Programs

Where do correctional officers stand in relation to the chaplain and religious programs?

• Correctional officers should encourage inmates to take advantage of the religious opportunities offered to them.

• When supervising religious services, officers should keep supervision activity to the respectful minimum necessary to ensure order.

• When speaking about a chaplain, officers should always use the chaplain's proper title, e.g., Father (for a Catholic chaplain); Reverend (for a Protestant chaplain); Rabbi (for a Jewish chaplain); etc.

• Officers should never make any derogatory statements about an inmate consulting a chaplain or attending services.

• Officers should call the chaplain's attention to inmates who seem to have personal or family problems.

Religion can play an important part in the institutional experience for an inmate. It is important that officers realize the significance of religious programs, and the chaplain's essential place in the institution.

## Drug Abuse Programs

Given the increasing number of drug offenders coming into this nation's prisons, the need for treatment programs has never been greater. While there are many different kinds of programs available, and it is impossible to discuss any of them at length in a handbook of this type, there are a few general points that are worth noting.

First, many drug offenders have already been through many treatment programs before; they know the ropes, and they often use the program for their own purposes. Correctional staff should give proper respect to the professional opinions of counselors and other staff regarding inmate change and program guidelines, but they should not relax security or supervision rules appropriate to that institution. Inmates involved in any program of any type must be required to obey the institution's rules, and staff must enforce those rules.

Second, in some past drug treatment programs, professional staff have let the inmates enforce the rules of the group or unit. This can lead to inmate control of the program, a totally unacceptable practice.

Third, no areas are off-limits to staff or free from staff searches. Correctional officers must continue to make sure that weapons, escape paraphernalia, and drugs are not hidden in the program areas.

Finally, staff should always be aware of the need to devote additional supervision and search activity to a group of drug offenders. It is never safe to assume that inmates in a drug treatment program genuinely want to quit using drugs. Regular procedures should always apply, and additional attention to these procedures is often advisable.

A sound visiting program is essential to the successful operation of any correctional institution. Frequent visits by family members and friends help maintain family and community ties, lessen the negative psychological consequences of confinement, and in some cases generate attitudes that are important for successful reentry into the community following confinement. In addition, visiting strengthens inmate morale and eases tensions and management problems. Other visitors can include lawyers, parole advisors who assist in release planning, and members of the clergy who may provide counseling to help resolve family problems.

In recognizing these issues, courts have consistently upheld inmates' right to receive visitors, while granting wide discretion to correctional administrators as to how the visitation program should be conducted. However, certain features or practices are common to most visiting programs.

As a general policy, contact visiting is preferred, that is, visiting in an area where inmates can actually be in contact with their visitors without any physical barriers. The use of noncontact visiting for high-security and some jail cases is still a valid strategy, but it is far less common.

### Visiting Hours

Visiting hours should not be overly restrictive. The number of visitors an inmate may receive, and the length of visits, should be limited only to the institution's schedule, the available visiting space, and staffing limitations. Most institutions permit visiting on Saturdays, Sundays, and holidays. Because restrictions may be a hardship to some families and other visitors, more generous, flexible visiting hours are strongly encouraged. This means maximizing visiting opportunities and accommodating visitors who are unable to schedule their visits during the institution's regular visiting hours. Ordinarily the caseworker or some other staff member, not the visiting room officer, approves these exceptions.

Because family members are the most frequent visitors, the institution's policy should permit visits by children. This further strengthens family ties, which can be strained during confinement, and reduces any child care problems associated with visits. This practice can make visiting more frequent and convenient, and less expensive.

### Processing Procedures

Visitors should be received in a waiting room or lobby area that has a hospitable, nonthreatening atmosphere. Their arrival should be recorded in the necessary records. Other processing typically includes checking identities, advising visitors of contraband

## A sound visiting program is essential to the successful operation of any correctional institution.

regulations, searching them, and then notifying the inmate of their arrival. Provision must be made to store visitors' prohibited personal belongings.

Visitors who refuse to follow these procedures, who are under the influence of alcohol or some other substance, or who are not properly dressed may be refused access to the institution under applicable local procedures.

Body searches of inmates, and a search of all clothing worn into the visiting room, are conducted both before and after visits to ensure that no contraband has been passed during the visit. These searches should be conducted in a suitable private area. Most institutions limit the items that may come and go into the visiting room, and others issue special visiting room clothing, or jumpsuits, to reduce the possibility of concealing contraband.

Private rooms are provided, whenever possible, for visits with attorneys. This permits the free exchange of confidential information and documents necessary in privileged communications between attorneys and their clients. These areas may also serve as secure visiting rooms for inmates who present serious escape risks or whose behavior may be disruptive, although in those cases, direct staff supervision is mandatory, whereas in attorney-client visiting no supervision is permitted that would allow overhearing any conversations.

## Visiting Program Staff

Visiting programs are usually supervised by two or three full-time members of the correctional staff, and should be carried out in the least intrusive manner possible. Although some surveillance can be provided by moving about the visiting room, there should also be a fixed staff post in the visiting room that affords good visibility of the entire area. Surveillance of the visiting room should not be carried out solely through the use of closed-circuit television or audio monitors, but they can greatly help in providing additional surveillance capability.

## Special Arrangements

Some visits require special arrangements. For example, visitors for inmates in segregation units or the infirmary can be escorted to these areas where the visits can be held in appropriately supervised rooms or existing multiuse space. In the case of inmates in segregation, the administration may also choose to use the private visiting rooms in the main visiting area. Whatever arrangements are made, these inmates should be properly restrained while being moved, and in some cases, the restraints may have to be left on for the visit. Special search procedures may also be necessary for any visitors moving into the secure compound for a visit of this type.

# Mail

While not a program in the strict sense, the importance of inmates' correspondence with relatives and friends becomes greatly magnified in a correctional setting. Frequent visiting by inmates' families is not always feasible because of such factors as cost and location. Thus, correspondence should be encouraged between inmates and their families, friends, and other associates. Moreover, correspondence between inmates and their attorneys and the courts must be assured. This usually requires

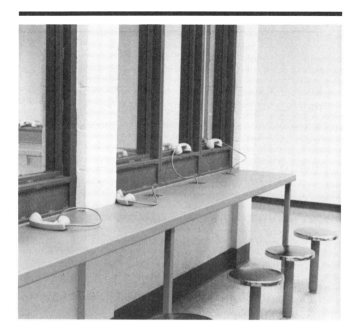

special handling, adding to the complexities of the mail operation.

The mail room is the area through which all incoming and outgoing mail passes. A major part of the mail room staff's work is opening, inspecting, and sorting incoming inmate mail. There are usually comprehensive rules and regulations governing incoming correspondence, based on the need to maintain security. The control of contraband entering the institution is a major concern. Unless incoming inmate mail is opened and inspected, staff lose control of contraband entering through the mail.

Incoming and outgoing legal mail and other privileged correspondence usually requires special handling. Such mail must be logged, and frequently must be opened in the mail room in the inmate's presence.

Catalog orders and packages delivered under approved programs also require special handling. This includes removing the contents from all packaging, searching the incoming material thoroughly, and giving only the contents to the inmate. The wrapping material is a prime location for contraband, and should be disposed of outside the institution. Unsearched packages should never be brought inside the compound, and for that reason the package area should not be deep inside the compound. Staff packages should receive special attention as well, with only the designated staff member permitted to pick up and search the package in the package area.

Inmates generally drop outgoing mail in a box in their housing unit, where it is collected daily and brought to the mail room. Outgoing inmate mail is not usually inspected as closely as incoming, but certain inmates or certain types of mail may receive special attention. In many institutions, the mail is no longer censored, and is just spot-checked for codes or other obvious attempts to breach security.

To the degree possible, administrative mail should be kept separate from inmate mail. This can usually be arranged with the postal authorities. Staff members should be assigned individual locked mailboxes.

Inmates should be absolutely prohibited from working in the mail room.

## Issues in Program Supervision

In addition to drug treatment groups, all program activities require supervision. Every institution will have its own layout and procedures, which will create unique supervision issues. However, a few tips are applicable to most situations:

• No program area is off-limits to staff supervision or searches.

• Officers assigned to supervise inmate spectators of such recreational activities should not become so engrossed in the game as to neglect their job of custodial supervision of all inmates.

• If outside visitors or players are present, care should be taken to prevent unnecessary contact between inmates and visitors.

• Officers should ensure that program activity is carried out only during the time specified.

• Staff should be careful not to give too much authority to inmate clerks or assistants in program areas.

• Except for open yard time and similar activities, most programs will have approved participant lists, which can be checked against callout sheets or other tally systems; correctional staff assigned to posts that control traffic into program areas need to be aware of those systems and ready to stop unauthorized inmates.

• Officers need to be aware of unusual traffic into or out of an area; large numbers of a minority group at unusual times, or the mass exit of many inmates, can signal a potential problem. These kinds of subtle signs should be reported to supervisors immediately.

• Program areas can be used as "stashes" for contraband, escape paraphernalia, or weapons; searches of inmates moving in and out of program areas are important, as are regular searches of the area itself.

• Staff offices should be periodically searched, particularly when they are shared by inmate clerks.

• Some programs have mail and packages delivered to them from outside organizations; these items should go through the regular institution search process, and inmates should never be sent to pick up packages of this type. Similarly, any outgoing correspondence for a program should be carefully controlled by staff, and subjected to normal institution mail processing.

## Locked-Unit Programs

Delivery of program services to locked units is an important issue. Staff working these units often do not understand that there are important management and legal reasons for offering medical, recreational, educational, and sometimes even vocational programs to inmates in locked status.

The operation of these programs is always a security concern. The movement of inmates to the program, or program materials to inmates' cells, is a time-consuming activity. Searches and application of restraints are necessary if an inmate is moved out of a cell, and the additional materials in inmate cells demand that more time be spent in cell searches. These are, however, necessary programs, and correctional officers should carry them out in accord with policy.

One absolute rule for all locked-unit programs is that inmates participating in them receive no extra privileges, nor are they relieved from the necessary security precautions that apply to all inmates in the unit. Program participation is commendable, and in most systems there are ways for inmates to eventually be recognized for it. However, the risks of relaxing procedures in the high-security setting are far too great. Even if inmates were not personally inclined to take advantage of a staff member's relaxation of procedure, they would quickly come under pressure from other inmates to do so.

## Special Issues in Camp Operations

Camp programs are often very similar to those operated inside secure facilities; the delivery of basic services to inmates differs very little. The trap that correctional staff can easily fall into in camp operations is to begin to believe that the inmates do not need the same kind of supervision that those inside the secure compound require.

In fact, in some respects, the lack of a wall or fence means that more personal supervision may actually be required. In the program area, it is just as important at a camp to supervise groups, search areas, and be alert for unhealthy interactions. Since it is so much easier to introduce drugs, alcohol, and other contraband, the need for searches of all areas, including program departments, is greater.

## Summary

The constructive use of an inmate's time should be an integral part of every correctional program. Participation in worthwhile programs can offer inmates a feeling of achievement, and aid them in acquiring skills that can help them live lawfully in the community.

Programs and security must not be viewed as separate systems, but as two important parts of the institutional structure. Correctional officers can assist inmates in their program activities by providing proper supervision, and by advising other staff when inmate conduct may require special attention.

*APPLICABLE ACA STANDARDS*

Academic and Vocational Education: 3-4410 to 3-4422
Inmate Work Programs: 3-4394 to 3-4409
Library, Recreation, and Inmate Activities: 3-4423 to 3-4428, and 3-4447 to 3-4453
Religious Services: 3-4454 to 3-4463
Social Services: 3-4380 to 3-4388

# 14

## Parole and Release

The vast majority of inmates who serve time in correctional institutions are released early under some form of parole or other community supervision. In many states, a parole board or commission decides when to return inmates to the community. In some states, in addition to parole, inmates may be granted what is called a mandatory release; they are released automatically after serving their maximum sentence, minus credit for "good time." In both cases, inmates who are released early are subject to a period of supervision by a parole officer.

While under supervision in the community, the inmate must report regularly to the supervising parole officer, who in some cases may also serve as a probation officer for offenders who are under probation from the court. They must receive approval for their proposed residence, job, and other details of their personal life, and may be required to participate in special counseling or drug testing programs. If they do not follow these restrictions, or if they violate the law in any way, they can be sent back to prison.

### Determinate Sentencing

There is a move in some U.S. states, and most recently in the federal system, to do away with parole and good-time credits, and move toward what is called a determinate sentencing procedure. This shift is a result of many complex political and criminal justice decisions, and is tending already to result in longer terms being served, making release an even longer term prospect for many inmates. For staffs working in systems with such a sentencing structure, some of this chapter will not apply, but much of it will be good background information on how other correctional systems operate.

### The Role of Institutional Staff

Correctional staff in every part of the institution can help inmates prepare to return to society. They can try to direct inmates into activities that may help them in lawful functioning upon release, including education, training, and self-improvement programs. With the availability of these programs and a properly motivated inmate, preparation for release can begin the day an inmate enters the institution.

Normally, when inmates are committed, institutional staff work with them to identify problem areas in their background, and to encourage them to enter programs that may help them deal with those problems. Probation officers' pre-sentence reports provide the background of case information from which the institution unit teams or classification staff can begin to work to develop this program with the inmate. The unit team or classification staff evaluate other records from custodial, treatment, educational, and industrial areas.

Institutional staff prepare reports about the inmates' program participation that are given to the paroling authority as part of the parole decision process. Program participation is one of the factors usually considered by the paroling authority in its decision. Inmates who are going to be released mandatorily do not ordinarily have these kinds of reports reviewed by any releasing authority.

### Pre-release Programs

Pre-release programs take different forms in different states. Most programs are designed to educate inmates about the social and economic

their sentences. Officers, though, should be cautious about being overly flexible about rule enforcement when the inmate soon will be released into the community. Disciplinary regulations still apply to all inmates at all times, until their sentences are completed.

Although this is not a complete list, correctional systems using temporary release programs include many of the following features:

- Written procedures, including careful screening and selection procedures that ensure public safety
- Written rules of conduct and sanctions
- A system of supervision to minimize inmate abuse of program privileges
- A complete record-keeping system
- A system for evaluating program effectiveness
- Efforts to obtain community cooperation and support

## The Institutional Parole Officer

Some institutions have institutional parole officers (often classification staff members), who act as liaisons between the classification committee or unit team, the parole authority, and supervising field staff. Other correctional systems have caseworkers who serve this purpose.

Institutional parole officers interpret parole policies for the staff and inmates, help develop pre-parole training programs, and counsel inmates during their incarceration. Soon after inmates are received in the institution, the parole officer may request additional information from field parole staff, if the probation pre-sentence reports are incomplete. This may result in a field officer visiting an inmate's family or former employer. This effort also can ensure that these important contacts are maintained, and help prepare the inmate's family and community for his or her eventual release.

Most parole authorities require that releasing inmates have, at a minimum, a job and a place to live when they are paroled. For that reason, when an inmate is eligible for parole review, the parole officer

realities of life outside the institution, and the agencies and services that can help them adjust. As part of these programs, lectures and discussions address the concerns of soon-to-be-released inmates, counselors focus on their particular needs, and parole officers may visit them.

Ideally, inmates in pre-release programs gradually receive less supervision as their level of responsibility increases. However, graduated release must at all times be consistent with public safety and the security level assigned to the inmate. When appropriate, inmates may be released under carefully controlled programs to work, study, and visit their family and community. In many institutions, inmates who are considered minimum-security risks and who are within several months of release are carefully selected to participate in community-based programs, which ease their transition from prison to the community. In some systems, low-risk offenders may be allowed short-term releases through brief furloughs to seek employment commitments or prospective residences. To provide these offenders with a more normal and relaxed living situation shortly before their release, other administrators permit inmates nearing release to live in separate quarters within the institution.

In these programs, inmate progress is evaluated according to behavior, rather than to the provisions of or caseworker helps develop a parole plan for consideration by the parole authority. This often will involve sending the proposed parole plan to the field parole staff for investigation and approval. The caseworker or parole officer often attends parole hearings, and may later explain in some instances why an inmate was denied release. After parole is granted, the officer helps explain the parole conditions to the parolee.

## The Field Parole Officer

The purpose of field parole officers is to guide and assist the parolee and others concerned with that individual's adjustment.

Shortly after inmates arrive at the institution— long before they are eligible for parole—field officers may be asked to investigate them to supplement the records received by the institution from the probation department and the court. In addition, they might contact the inmate's family to discuss immediate and long-range problems resulting from the commitment, referring them to agencies where they can obtain assistance. This officer can, therefore, help lay the foundation with family, friends, and former

*Most pre-release programs are designed to educate inmates about the social and economic realities of life outside the institution, and the agencies and services that can help them adjust.*

employers for the inmate's future return to and acceptance in the community.

In some agencies, field officers visit the institution periodically to interview potential parolees and to help them maintain important familial and community contacts. After release is granted, officers investigate the living and employment plan forwarded by the institutional parole officer, and either recommend or disapprove it, submitting their decision and a more suitable plan to the board.

These officers are often members of a field service agency actually within the corrections department, and use formal procedures for supervising inmates. Parole officers monitor parolees at home and in the community through surveillance, counsel them on personal matters, and solicit other community services for them by helping them find other treatment services. These procedures may require staff to assign parolees a level of supervision based on their risk to the community and their need for services and assistance. While on parole, offenders are often

limited or controlled for a trial period to determine whether they are willing and able to live within the laws of the free community.

Ideally, the officer is aware at all times of the parolee's whereabouts, activities, and conduct. Parolees often consult their parole officer about problems involving their job, family, residence, health, expenses, or pressures posed by former crime partners. Individuals whose behavior becomes threatening to society or to themselves are immediately returned to custody. In many (though not all) states, parole officers may arrest or cause the arrest of any parolee when there is reason to believe that the parole conditions have been violated.

Parole officers must submit a full report of any alleged infractions to the parole authority, which reviews it and determines whether the individual must return to the institution for a hearing that could result in parole revocation. If a parolee has absconded and cannot be taken into custody, the officer will request that the parole status be suspended immediately and a warrant be issued for the parolee's arrest. If parole is subsequently revoked, the time after the suspension order does not count toward the completion of the parole period or the maximum sentence.

When an officer believes an individual no longer requires supervision and the parole administrative staff concurs, the officer may submit a recommendation for discharge to the paroling authority. The authority is generally authorized by statute to release parolees before their maximum sentence dates, or to at least reduce the reporting requirements for the rest of the sentence.

## Summary

Correctional officers as well as other employees play a major role in preparing inmates for release, whether it is on parole or not. This is best accomplished by helping inmates develop positive attitudes and behaviors necessary for a law-abiding life within the free community.

During the 1970s through the 1980s, the concept of parole was seriously questioned. Some states severely restricted, or even eliminated, discretionary parole release. However, parole is a strong component of correctional systems in many jurisdictions, and even where abolished, it will still be a factor in the community supervision of many inmates sentenced before the parole laws were changed.

*APPLICABLE ACA STANDARDS*

Release Preparation and Temporary Release:
    3-4389 to 3-4393

# 15

## Public Relations and Citizen Involvement

**M**aintaining the public's full confidence and respect is critical to corrections receiving necessary financial and other resources. Prisons, reformatories, and other institutions are performing public service functions with public funds, and citizens have a right to know how they are operated and how their tax monies are spent. The level of public support for corrections can decrease rapidly, or even vanish, when headlines result from mismanagement, disturbances, or general inmate discontent. Open relations with the community and the media can greatly aid in achieving public understanding and support.

By the same token, prison riots in the last several decades have also clearly reflected that inmates were convinced the public knew little or nothing of their plight—real or imagined. As a result, inmates believed that drastic action was needed to alert the public to their demands. A policy of openness about public information about the institution can help prevent such potentially disruptive situations.

### The Value of Public Education

Good institutional public relations is really just public education. If the average citizen had an accurate picture of what corrections is about, what prison staff do, what kind of inmates they deal with, and what resources are actually available, there would be far fewer public concerns about prison operations, and probably more resources devoted to them. The image that most citizens have about prisons is shaped to a large degree by James Cagney and Clint Eastwood movies and the sensationalistic stories carried in the press and the electronic media when there is a riot or escape.

Other factors that affect how the public views

prisons are within correctional staff control. For example, telephone contacts and correspondence with the public affect how the institution is regarded; discourteous treatment in the course of a telephone call or the lack of a response to a letter of inquiry can reinforce an already negative image. A taxpayer who is disgruntled because of inconsiderate treatment at the hands of an institutional employee can cause untold damage to the institution's reputation and the professional status of its employees.

To a certain degree, public images about corrections are also shaped by what local citizens see in the lives and behavior of institutional staff. Careless speech, negative comments about inmates, improper use of the uniform, impolite and discourteous personal relationships—all of these day-to-day elements can contribute to poor public relations. They certainly can damage or destroy in a moment the hard work of many others who are trying to upgrade the public's view of corrections.

### The Media

Mass media sources are the most common avenues for information, and yet correctional agencies traditionally have been reluctant to allow the press into institutions, or to allow inmates to have media contacts. However, a series of court cases in the last several decades have reinforced the principle that inmates' First Amendment rights include some form of access to the media. As a result, with the public's increased interest in correctional institutions, it is no surprise that inmates have made more demands to communicate directly to the public, or that the press has sought to report more fully on the activities and conditions of prison life.

Most agencies have a well-developed policy that

regulates how and when an inmate can write to the media, receive an in-person media interview, or make telephone calls to media representatives. All employees should familiarize themselves with these regulations to ensure that they do not violate a policy that is based on an important constitutional right.

Allowing the media to have access to correctional institutions should be more than just complying with court decisions—it can be a positive management tool. By permitting media representatives to come in prisons, see the programs and services that are offered, and watch staff do their jobs, correctional administrators can easily neutralize many of inmates' usually groundless claims about brutality and subhuman living conditions. When local reporters are familiar with the prison "beat," and know what actual living conditions are in the institution, they are far less likely to sensationalize the raw allegations of a discontented inmate, attorney, or outside support group. While a far more difficult task, to the degree that the national media can be convinced of the integrity and humanity of prison operations, fewer negative stories will appear at that level.

## The Role of the Correctional Officer

In most cases, the line correctional officer will not have direct contact with the media, and will be guided

*Maintaining the public's full confidence and respect is critical to corrections receiving necessary financial and other resources.*

by policies of the institution on what to do if contacted by the media. However, there are some important areas to remember.

### Public Information Functions

In most states and in the federal prison system, policy and statutes limit who may release information about inmates and institutional operations. These restrictions are often tied to legal limits on information disclosure about individual inmates. As a result, almost all institutions and agencies have a designated public information office, or a public information officer who is the only person authorized to release information about the organization. Line staff should be aware of the limits their particular agency places on employees in this regard, so that if they are approached with a request for information about the

institution by a reporter or a member of the public, they are familiar with what they may and may not say. When in doubt about the appropriate response, it is best to say nothing, and to either refer the person to the public information officer or seek advice from a supervisor.

## Media Tours

Media tours can be an excellent way for getting out information about the institution and its programs. There is no question that most reporters, editors, and others in the media are under-informed about corrections. When they receive letters from inmates claiming severe abuses or inhumane living conditions, they have no frame of reference. Tours and regular open house sessions for public leaders help neutralize this factor. Officers who assist in institutional tours can be helpful by responding to questions about institutional routines, but they should refer questions about agency policies or individual inmates to a supervisor or public information officer.

## Ethics and Relationships with Ex-Inmates and Inmate Families

The entire subject of ethics is an important one, and it is covered in some detail in the ACA Code of Ethics (see the inside back cover of this guide). But in addition to the topics covered in the Code, there are

*If the average citizen had an accurate picture of what corrections is about, what prison staff do, what kind of inmates they deal with, and what resources are actually available, there would be far fewer public concerns about prison operations, and probably more resources devoted to them.*

several points that require additional explanation regarding the specific relationship between inmates and staff.

Most institutions have a clear policy against any kind of business dealings between staff and inmates. This is to prevent staff becoming in any way obligated to inmates, and thereby being subject to extortion or pressure to bring in contraband, aid in an escape, or engage in some other improper or illegal activity.

Speaking bluntly, staff need to approach their relationships with inmates with a very healthy dose of skepticism, tempered by extreme caution. While it is perfectly appropriate for employees to give advice to inmates in professional areas in which they are qualified, there are no occasions where staff should approach inmates for advice of any kind, or share with them their personal affairs. Those situations not only can be the start of an obligatory relationship, but can provide the inmate with personal information about employees that can later be used against them and the institution.

The classic example is that of an inmate learning from an officer about financial difficulties, and the inmate offering first financial advice and then direct assistance, if only the officer will do a simple favor. The same strategy can be employed if an inmate learns about an employee's marital problems and attempts to exploit the employee's emotional turmoil.

There are many variations on this theme, but in the final analysis, staff members who get too "close" to inmates are at great risk of compromising not only themselves, but institutional security.

Family and community relationships can be just as complicated. In many small towns, the families of inmates, and ex-inmates themselves, may live, work, and at times be involved in civic and social functions with institutional staff. These relationships, while not always bad, have a great potential for problems.

In general, most agencies will have a policy that guides staff on the limits on these kinds of contacts. However, as a rule, business and other financial relationships with even an ex-inmate would be considered a particularly serious concern, as would any personal contact of any kind with the spouse or family of a current inmate.

This is a sensitive area in which there is not total agreement, primarily because of the increasing use of community correctional programs that keep offenders in or near their home communities. However, the rule of thumb for all of these situations is to follow agency policies and talk to supervisory staff; when in doubt about a particular situation, it is probably best not to be involved.

### Drug-Free Staff

In a time when American society is highly concerned with drug abuse, correctional institutions should be as drug-free as modern security can make them. But in addition to the inmates, staff also must be drug-free.

There was a time when such a statement would have been unnecessary—when drug use was not a part of middle America or the portion of the work force that corrections draws on for its staff. Unfortunately, this is no longer the case, as many Americans in all walks of life have experimented with drugs of some type at some point in their life.

There are several reasons for prison staff members to be drug-free. First, in most cases, drug use is illegal, and correctional staff are sworn to uphold the law. Second, in the correctional setting it is critical that all staff members be fully alert and unimpaired in their ability to act; the lives of inmates and fellow staff members literally depend on it. Third, in institutions where there are armed posts, a drug-impaired person is a risk to not only other staff, but to the public and inmates. Next, if inmates detect a person who is drug-dependent (and they very easily can), they will attempt to blackmail that person for personal gain, and ultimately compromise the institution's security. In most cases, they eventually also turn in the "dirty" staff members when they are done "using" them, often to gain some small additional benefit when they finally expose the staff members' cooperation. Finally, the damage to the institution's public image, and to that of corrections as well, is very great when a drug-abusing staff member is finally found out, and fired and/or prosecuted.

### Personal Conduct and Appearance

The matter of staff members' personal conduct and appearance ties in with the drug issue. If prison employees are involved in disruptive behavior in the community, if they are alcohol abusers, dress disreputably, or otherwise are not good citizens, those

impressions will inevitably rub off on the institution. People will say, "Well, if that's the kind of person they have working out there, all those stories I've heard must be true." Every employee is a walking ambassador for corrections, a representative of the institution itself, the agency, and corrections as a profession.

Community involvement on the part of employees is another part of this picture. If employees are contributing to their community in a positive way—managing ball teams or being active in civic organizations or church affairs, for instance—they will reinforce the thought that the institution and its staff are good members of the community, and that corrections is positive.

## Citizen Involvement in Prison Activities

Good institutional programming often involves structured inmate contacts with desirable people from outside the prison. Some jurisdictions have a citizen advisory or community relations board for each institution. These groups can provide information on, and referrals to, community programs that can benefit inmates, such as work and study release, recreation activities, and theater groups. Citizen involvement and volunteer programs can generate a wide variety of services for inmates, both during their confinement and after their release. These activities may include sports programs, volunteer tutor sessions, and religious counseling.

Security precautions are necessary while permitting these contacts; depending on the institution, staff escorts or supervision may be required. Most locations have a screening and orientation process for those involved, and provide necessary staff escorts or supervision, depending on the activity or area of the institution involved. The institution can contribute to the development of positive community relationships by providing adequate facilities and streamlined procedures for these joint inside-outside activities.

Inmates should be aware of volunteer services and the nature of those services. Attempts should be made to see that inmates understand volunteers' role and the limits of their authority.

## Community and Public Service Activities

Institutions and suitably classified, low-risk inmates have carried out many community and public service programs. These programs not only help the community, but also give inmates a greater sense of self-worth and membership in the outside world. Examples include inmates running marathon races inside institutions to raise money for local charities through community sponsors, Jaycee organizations in prisons assisting outside Jaycee groups in civic activities, institutions providing fire-fighting crews for local fire emergencies, and even direct inmate manpower for civic improvement projects such as improving park and recreation facilities.

Inmates at forestry camps frequently are used for fire fighting and for searching for children or adults lost in the woods. Inmate pharmacists from these camps sometimes give first aid to local residents when regular medical services are not available. Inmates

have been released to help communities in flood and hurricane emergencies.

Inmates from many institutions donate toys they have repaired to needy children at Christmas time. They frequently donate products of their craft work, such as ashtrays, lamps, bookends, and custom-made jewelry, to members of the clergy for distribution to various church groups. The inmate stamp club at one correctional institution donated approximately 300 stamp albums with United States cancellations and 300 packets of assorted cancellations to orphanages that sponsor stamp clubs.

Inmates of many institutions have adopted children through organizations devoted to finding suitable homes and sponsors for underprivileged children around the world. The adopting individual or group contributes as little as $15 a month, out of which the child receives an outright grant. The remainder is used for food and clothing packages, translation of letters, medical services, and education.

Inmates in several state facilities organize magnetic tape-recording programs. Hundreds of books at every level of interest—philosophy, religion, literature, history, mathematics, and science--are taped when requested. In most cases, the sponsor organization is responsible for supplying the equipment to the correctional institution, and in many

*To a certain degree, public images about corrections are shaped by what local citizens see in the lives and behavior of institutional staff.*

cases receives assistance from such interested groups as service clubs and business or charitable organizations.

## Summary

Good public information activity and productive citizen involvement are major factors in the support that a correctional institution receives. Correctional officers have the opportunity to play a role in this function by presenting a professional image of both their work and the correctional institution, as well as understanding and facilitating the formal programs that work toward that goal.

*APPLICABLE ACA STANDARDS*

Citizen Involvement and Volunteers: 3-4111 to 3-4119

# Index

Activities, Inmate Recreation and, 112–114
Addiction, Drug Abuse or, 90–92, 115
AIDS, 86–88
Alcoholics, Inmate, 92
Appearance and Personal Conduct, Officers', 127
Armed Supervision, 51
Asthma and Other Chronic Illnesses, 90

Body Searches, 41, 102
Bombs, 65

Camp Programs, 119
Cardiopulmonary Resuscitation (CPR), 85–86
Chaplains, 114–115
Citizen Involvement, 127–128
Civil Disturbances, 66
Classification, 104–106
Commissary, 74
Communications, 47
Community and Public Service, 128–129
Contraband and Searches, 40–41
Contraband, Disposal of, 42
Control Center, 38
Correspondence, 117–118
Counseling, Inmate, 112
Count Methods, 39–40
Courts, 4, 6–7

Diabetes, 89–90
Diets, Special, 72
Dining Areas, 72–73
Disasters, 68–69
Discharge Areas, Loading and, 51
Disciplinary Procedures, 27–30
Disorders, Inmate Personality, 95–96
Disturbances, Civil, 66
Disturbances, Personality Pattern, 96–97
Disturbances, Personality Trait, 96–97
Drug Abusers and Addicts, 90–92, 115

Educational Programs and Vocational Training, 110–111
Emergency Plans and Procedures, 56, 58–69

Epilepsy, 88–89
Equipment Control, Tool and, 44
Escapes, 37

Field Parole Officer, The, 122–123
Fires, 63–64
Firearms, ACA Standards for, 56
Firearms Training, 52–53
Firing Positions, 53–54
Food Preparation, 71–72
Food Service, ACA Standards for, 72
Food Service Items, 44
Food Storage, 71
Force, Use of Deadly, 51–52

Gas, 54
Gases, Riot Control, 54
Gate Entrances, Pedestrian, 35–36
Gate Entrances, Vehicular, 35–36

Hair Care, 80
High-security Risk Inmates, 47
History, Correctional, 5–6
HIV, 86–88
Hospital Equipment, 45
Hostages, 36, 65–66
Housing Unit Search, 42
Hygiene, Sanitation and, 76–80

Information Gathering, 23–24
Information Sharing, 23–24
Inmates, Restraint and Recapture, 63
Inspections, Sanitation, 76–77
Inspections, Security, 46–47, 60
Institutional Parole Officer, The, 121–122
Issuing Orders, 21–22

Job Action, Employee, 67–68

Key Control, Lock and, 45–46

Laundry Programs, 79–80

Law Enforcement, 4
Law, Inmate Violation of, 28
Lawsuits, Federal Constitutional, 15–17
Lawsuits, Inmate, 13, 15–17
Legal Definitions, 14
Legal Issues, Overview, 12–18
Legal Resources, Inmate Access to, 17–18
Lighting, 37
Line Counts, 39–40
Litigation, Reducing Possibility of, 18
Loading and Discharge Areas, 51
Lock and Key Control, 45–46
Locked-unit Procedures, 30–32
Locked-unit Status, Administrative, 29–30
Locked-unit Status, Disciplinary, 30

Mail, 117–118
Meal Service, 72
Media Relations, 59, 124–126
Medical Trips, 84
Medication Issues, 83–84
Mentally Ill Inmates, 94–100
Mentally Retarded Inmates, 99–100
Minor Violations and Major Infractions of Rules, 27–28
Movement and Count Methods, 38–40
Moves, Forced Cell, 56–57

Neuroses, Inmate, 94

Observing Inmates, 22
Orders, Issuing, 21–22
Orders, Post, 23, 35
Orientation, 102–106
Outcounts, 39–40

Parole, 120–123
Parole Officer, The Field, 122–123
Parole Officer, The Institutional, 121–122
Pedestrian Gate Entrances, 35–36
Perimeter Searches, 24
Personality Disorders, Inmate, 95–96
Personality Pattern Disturbances, 96–97
Physical Plant Design, 38–39
Post-riot Activities, 61–62
Pre-release Programs, 120–121
Programming, 108–119
Programs, Locked-unit, 118–119
Property, 77
Prosecution, 4
Psychoses, Inmate, 94–95
Public Relations, 124–129
Public Service, Community and, 128–129

Reception and Orientation Activities, 102–106
Records, 23, 30, 45, 87
Recreation and Inmate Activities, 112–114
Release Preparation, 120–121
Religious Programs, 114–115
Report Writing, 18, 27–28
Responsibilities of the Correctional Officer, 8–9

Restraints, 54–55
Riots, 60–62

Sanitation and Hygiene, 76–80
Searches, Body, 41, 102
Searches, Contraband, 40–41
Searches, Housing Unit, 42
Searches, Inmate, 41
Searches, Locked-unit, 32
Searches, Perimeter, 24
Searches, Vehicle, 42–43
Searches, Visitor, 43–44
Security Features, External, 34–37
Security, Internal, 37–39
Segregation, Inmate, 28–32
Self-Defense Techniques, Unarmed, 55–56
Sexual Behavior in Correctional Settings, 25–27
Sick Call in Prison, 83
Social Services, 109–110
Staff Recall in Emergency Plans, 69
Storage, Drugs, 83–84
Storage, Food, 71
Storage, Tool, 44
Storage, Weapon, 50–51
Strikes, Inmate Work/Food, 66–67
Suicide Risk, Inmate, 98–99
Supervision, Armed, 51
Supervision, Dining Area, 72–73
Supervision, Direct versus Indirect, 21
Supervision of Hospitals and Infirmaries, 84
Supervision of Housing Units, 22–23
Supervision of Special Units, 47–48
Supervision of Visiting Area, 116–117
Supervision of Work Details, 24
Supervision, Program, 118
Supplies, Food, 71
Surveillance, 24–25

Tool and Equipment Control, 44, 75
Towers, Walls, 34
Training, 9–10
Transportation, Inmate, 25

Unarmed Defense, 55–56
Use of Force, 50–57

Vehicular Gate Entrances, 35–36
Violation of Law, 28
Violations and Major Infractions of Rules, Minor, 27–28
Visibility, Fog/Reduced, 67
Visiting Area Search, 43–44
Visiting Program, 116–117
Visitor Searches, 43–44
Vocational Programming, 110
Vocational Training, Educational Programs and, 110–111

Waste Disposal and Pest Control, 79
Weapons, Storage, Upkeep, and Use of, 50–51
Work Details, Supervision of, 24
Work Programs, 111–112

# Code of Ethics

*The American Correctional Association expects of its members unfailing honesty, respect for the dignity and individuality of human beings, and a commitment to professional and compassionate service. To this end we subscribe to the following principles.*

Relationships with clients/colleagues/other professions/ the public—

- Members will respect and protect the civil and legal rights of all clients.
- Members will serve each case with appropriate concern for the client's welfare and with no purpose of personal gain.
- Relationships with colleagues will be of such character to promote mutual respect within the profession and improvement of its quality of service.
- Statements critical of colleagues or their agencies will be made only as these are verifiable and constructive in purpose.
- Members will respect the importance of all elements of the criminal justice system and cultivate a professional cooperation with each segment.
- Subject to the client's rights of privacy, members will respect the public's right to know, and will share information with the public with openness and candor.
- Members will respect and protect the right of the public to be safeguarded from criminal activity.

Professional conduct/practices—

- No member will use his or her official position to secure special privileges or advantages.
- No member, while acting in an official capacity, will allow personal interest to impair objectivity in the performance of duty.
- No member will use his or her official position to promote any partisan political purposes.
- No member will accept any gift or favor of such nature to imply an obligation that is inconsistent with the free and objective exercise of professional responsibilities.
- In any public statement, members will clearly distinguish between those that are personal views and those that are statements and positions on behalf of an agency.
- Members will be diligent in their responsibility to record and make available for review any and all case information that could contribute to sound decisions affecting a client or the public safety.
- Each member will report, without reservation, any corrupt or unethical behavior which could affect either a client or the integrity of the organization.
- Members will not discriminate against any client, employee, or prospective employee on the basis of race, sex, creed, or national origin.
- Members will maintain the integrity of private information; they will neither seek personal data beyond that needed to perform their responsibilities, nor reveal case information to anyone not having proper professional use for such.
- Any member who is responsible for agency personnel actions will make all appointments, promotions, or dismissals only on the basis of merit and not in furtherance of partisan political interests.

(Adopted August 1975 at the 105th Congress of Correction)

# Earn College Credits with ACA Correspondence Courses

*New!*

**B**eginning this fall, students completing ACA's correspondence courses will be able to earn college credits through Salve Regina University's credit by examination program.

**S**alve Regina University is an independent co-educational institution of higher learning located in Newport, Rhode Island. The University is fully accredited by the New England Association of Schools and Colleges. Credits earned through the University will be transferable to institutions of higher learning.

**T**he new credit by examination program gives corrections professionals at all levels a cost-effective way to further their education. They will not only better their job skills but also reduce their tuition and travel expenses.

**F**or more information about this exciting new program and its costs, call:
1-800-825-2665 or (301) 206-5059 (MD, DC, VA)

---

ACA correspondence courses provide a unique opportunity for corrections personnel to improve their job performance and promotion opportunities. These courses are also valuable classroom materials for trainers. Professional certificates are awarded by ACA on completion.

▮ **Motivating Correctional Staff** (#174)
Nonmembers $65.00; ACA members $52.00

▮ **Working With Special Needs Offenders** (#175)
Nonmembers $65.00; ACA members $52.00

▮ **Suicide Prevention in Custody** (#173)
*Intensive Study Course*
Nonmembers $33.00; ACA members $26.00

▮ **Correctional Officer** (#165)
Nonmembers $65.00; ACA members $52.00

▮ **Correctional Officer II** (#172)
Nonmembers $65.00; ACA members $52.00

▮ **Correctional Supervision** (#104)
Nonmembers $57.00; ACA members $46.00

▮ **Correctional Supervision II** (#171)
Nonmembers $57.00; ACA members $46.00

▮ **Report Writing** (#167)
Nonmembers $51.00; ACA members $41.00

▮ **Correctional Mid-Management Skills** (#168)
Nonmembers $65.00; ACA members $52.00

▮ **Correctional Food Service** (#166)
Nonmembers $51.00; ACA members $41.00

▮ **Legal Issues for Correctional Officers** (#170)
Nonmembers $57.00; ACA members $46.00

**ACA**

**Order toll-free**
**1-800-825-2665**

# Other Resources Available

## Vital Statistics in Corrections

Timely, accurate, statistical information about the salaries, benefits, education, and training of corrections staff and administrators in the U.S. Includes data about unions, employee groups, collective bargaining, budgets, institutional populations, recidivism rates, and jurisdictions under court order. New in this edition is information about jail populations and budgets; probation/parole, including aftercare service providers and number of adults on probation; female offender population for the past five years; and international rates of incarceration. *(1991, 74 pages, charts, graphs, tables, 0-929310-56-X)* **Item #123**

## Change, Challenge & Choices: Women's Role in Modern Corrections – Edited by Joann B. Morton, D.P.A.

An indispensable resource for managers, administrators, and educators, this thought-provoking compilation of articles by practitioners and academicians addresses critical issues associated with the expanded role of women in correctional employment. It incorporates information on management, legal, and training issues and makes recommendations for system improvement, employee enrichment, and future study. Also examines issues that directly affect line staff such as pregnancy, sexual harassment, changing employment opportunities, and what the future holds. *(1991, 124 pages, 0-929310-54-3)* **Item #322**

## Understanding Substance Abuse and Treatment

Developed by psychologists, corrections professionals, and drug abuse counselors, this comprehensive manual examines all types of substance abuse, symptoms of abuse, legal ramifications, and different forms of treatment. An overview of inmate addicts, treatment formats and techniques, and aftercare is included. Special sections discuss HIV/AIDS and the effects of addiction on family members. Combines the experiences of expert Federal Bureau of Prison staff. *(1992, 116 pages, 0-929310-73-X)* **Item #449**

## Correctional Law for the Correctional Officer –

### William C. Collins, J.D.

A handbook designed especially for the correctional officer working in an adult prison or jail. Answers officers' questions about the rights of inmates and staff and provides a basic understanding of the law. Explains legal liabilities and rights associated with: searches and seizures, use of force, punishment, AIDS, suicide, protections, religion, mail, visiting, and more. Review questions and answers for each chapter. *(1990, 140 pages, 0-929310-37-3)* **Item #429**

## Stress Management for Correctional Officers and Their Families – Frances E. Cheek, Ph.D.

Are you a victim of on-the-job stress? An expert explains the nature of correctional stress and provides a proven program of self-help techniques that can reduce physical and emotional wear and tear. Includes questionnaires as well as practical exercises for turning off the stress alarm. *(1984, 106 pages, 0-942974-63-8)* **Item #101**

American Correctional Association  8025 Laurel Lakes Court  Laurel, MD 20707-5075